The Equestrian Woman

The Equestrian Woman

By
ANN
MARTIN

PADDINGTON PRESS LTD

NEW YORK & LONDON

Library of Congress Cataloging in Publication Data

Martin, Ann.
  The equestrian woman.

  1. Horsewomen—Interviews. I. Title.
SF284.5.M37   798'.2'0922 [B]   78-24241
ISBN 0-448-22686-3   (U.S. and Canada only)
ISBN 0 7092 0516 3

Filmset in England by SX Composing Ltd., Rayleigh, Essex.
Printed and bound in the United States

Designed by Patricia Pillay

IN THE UNITED STATES
PADDINGTON PRESS
Distributed by
GROSSET & DUNLAP

IN THE UNITED KINGDOM
PADDINGTON PRESS

IN CANADA
Distributed by
RANDOM HOUSE OF CANADA LTD.

IN SOUTHERN AFRICA
Distributed by
ERNEST STANTON (PUBLISHERS) (PTY.) LTD.

IN AUSTRALIA AND NEW ZEALAND
Distributed by
A.H. & A.W. REED

Contents

Introduction

THROUGHOUT THE AGES women have always been associated with horses. Boadicea who died in A.D. 62 is said to have been the first British queen to maintain a racing stud. She is thought to have driven in chariot races and to have bred horses for export to Rome.

The beautiful Lady Godiva, wife of Earl Leofric, the Governor of Coventry during the eleventh century, rode her white horse naked through the streets of the town. She did this in order to persuade her husband to take off the tax on horses which affected most families very severely as they nearly all depended on these animals for transport.

Joan of Arc led her troops into battle on horseback, while Queen Elizabeth I, pale, frail, and glittering with jewels, in long, narrow bodices and countless skirts more suitable for a garden party, rode so fast that she continually alarmed the Master of the Horse, Lord Robert Dudley, who was responsible for her safety. Nevertheless, although protective and adoring, he fulfilled her wishes and wrote to the Earl of Sussex in Ireland informing him that the Queen would like some Irish horses dispatched to England as they might be faster than hers. He wrote: "She spareth not to try as fast as they can go. And I fear them much, yet she will prove them." She was frequently out riding when dispatches were brought to her and always read them on horseback.

The valiant American pioneer women sometimes traveled thousands of miles by horseback with their families from the Atlantic coast to settle in wild country. Many women, such as the tragic Elizabeth, Empress of Austria, have gained both happiness and solace in the hunting field.

In the twentieth century opportunities to ride are available for increasing numbers of women. And, despite the initial prejudice shown when 1957 European Champion Sheila Willcox, a Badminton winner in 1956, 1957 and 1958, tried to be accepted as an Olympic rider and was refused, Britain's Olympic three

The statue in Coventry commemorating Lady Godiva's famous ride through the streets. PHOTO: FINDLAY DAVIDSON

The pioneer of the British lady three day event riders, Sheila Willcox on Fair and Square, at Badminton, April 1969.
PHOTO: CYRIL DIAMOND

day event team included women in 1968, 1972 and 1976. The British 1975 European Championship silver-medal-winning team contained no men, consisting of Lucinda Prior-Palmer, Princess Anne, Sue Hatherly and Janet Hodgson. At the Tokyo Olympics in 1964, Helena Dupont who finished thirty-third overall on Mr. Wister – was a member of the U.S. Team that won the Three Day Event Silver Medals.

Baron Pierre de Coubertin, who founded the modern Olympic Games in 1892, would certainly not have approved, for he wrote: "Olympics with women would be incorrect, unpractical, uninteresting and not aesthetic." A principle of the Victorian era which would not be acceptable today.

Women were first permitted to ride in Olympic dressage in 1952 but were not allowed into the Olympic show-jumping arena until 1956, when the great Pat Smythe won a team bronze medal on Flanagan at Stockholm, together with Peter Robeson on Scorchin, and Wilf White on Nizefela.

In 1968 in Mexico City, Jane Bullen on Our Nobby and

European Horse Trials Championships in Luhmühlen, West
Germany in September 1975. The British team that collected the
silver medal: (left to right) Lucinda Prior-Palmer on Be Fair
(individual first), H.R.H. Princess Anne on Goodwill (individual
second), and Sue Hatherly on Harley. PHOTO: FINDLAY DAVIDSON

Germany's Liselott Linsenhoff became the first women to win
Olympic equestrian gold medals as members of their countries'
three day event and dressage teams respectively.

Today, women are highly regarded in many spheres of the
horse world. This book looks at over thirty contemporary
women who have risen to the top of their chosen field of equestrianism. They each reveal their personal experiences as horsewomen. Lucinda Prior-Palmer talks about her constant struggle
to improve her riding for three day eventing; Robyn Smith
tells of the problems of being a female jockey in a predominantly male sport; Princess Anne discusses how she combines
carrying out royal duties while training her horses for major
events. Three day eventers, show-jumpers, polo players,
jockeys, trainers, breeders, a groom, and many more, all talk
frankly about themselves and their horses and the unique
aspects of being equestrian women.

Lucinda Prior-Palmer

Three Day Eventer

ALTHOUGH SHE WAS ONLY twenty-four years old in 1978, Lucinda Prior-Palmer had already achieved the aura of a perennial star in the world of three day eventing. With victories in 1975 (Be Fair) and 1977 (George), she had become the first rider to win two European Championships and have three Badminton successes to her credit – 1973 (Be Fair), 1976 (Wideawake) and 1977 (George). The fact that she won Britain's premier three day event three times on different horses, makes her achievement self-explanatory. It is hard now to recall that over two decades ago in 1957 in Copenhagen, Sheila Willcox created history when, after lengthy argument and discussion in Britain as to whether women should be allowed to compete in the sport at international level, she won the European Championship with High and Mighty.

When Lucinda scored her first Badminton success in 1973 she sat afterward in the collecting ring with her constant companion, the King Charles spaniel, Oliver Plum, on her saddle. She could hardly believe that at only her second attempt she had conquered the best at Britain's foremost event.

Since that day she has matured into a very vital and coolly assessive world-class rider through a combination of utter determination, natural brilliance and continual hard work. Her forte remains her driving cross-country style, but as an extremely self-critical rider, she has left no stone unturned with visits to such trainers as show-jumping expert Bertalan de Nemethy of the United States Equestrian Team (U.S.E.T.), at Gladstone, New Jersey, and Herbert Rehbein in Germany

Britain's Lucinda Prior-Palmer and Be Fair on their way to winning the 1975 European Championship executing an extended trot during an excellent dressage test. PHOTO: FRANCIS SWIFT

where she completely restructured her dressage technique.

"When Be Fair finished fifth in the dressage at the Montreal Olympics at Bromont, I knew that although he'd never gone better he could still improve. But I didn't know how to ask him or what to do. I was very aware that if he'd had a better rider than I, he would have had a higher mark. I realized then that I must learn how to reach the next stage because I had ground to a halt and been stagnating. Everyone is trying to attain the same objective – reaching a time when the horse is not leaning on you, but moving off its hocks with the rider becoming part of the horse.

Lucinda Prior-Palmer and O.C.L.'s Village Gossip at Dauntsey Park, August, 1978. PHOTO: CYRIL DIAMOND

"In Germany, I learned that I had to go right back to the beginning and start again because the reason I could not progress further was that I had no basics. I realized that to progress I had to make an effort. I was not at stage two and ready for stage three, but hardly anywhere nearing stage one. This launched me on an uphill struggle and, although I've learned a new approach, every now and then I lapse into my old ways."

Lucinda's climb to the top began at Appleshaw House, a mellow Georgian building with a fine stableyard, near Andover, Hampshire. Here she lived with her late father, Major-General Erroll Prior-Palmer, C.B., a former top class polo player who had a distinguished army career in the 9th Lancers, and her mother, Lady Doreen, the youngest daughter of the second Marquess of Linlithgow. They both shared a love of horses and Lucinda had plenty of opportunities to learn to ride.

A sense of humor is a valuable asset where horses are concerned. Lucinda laughs a lot and one of her earliest memories is going to the nearby riding school when she was six years old. "Each Tuesday and Thursday Nanny Hockenhall took me for lessons from Mrs. Betty Skelton at Harroway House, three miles from Appleshaw. I used to ride pillion on her bicycle until one day we met Mr. Plod, the policeman who said, 'Madam, you are breaking the law taking a little girl on the back of your bike, it's far too dangerous.' After that we had to change our mode of transport and go by bus."

Soon she was gaining experience with a series of her own ponies, some of whom would jump and some of whom wouldn't unless very strongly persuaded. She became a member of the Royal Artillery Pony Club and went to camp. Eventually she had a fine, gray, thoroughbred-Connemara cross pony called Sea Sway. This pony was found by Suzanne Pennefeather who is now married to Ireland's leading international show-jumper Eddie Macken. She was green as grass, but jumped like a stag and gave Lucinda her introduction to one day events. At their first attempt Lucinda fell off at the fifth cross-country fence when Sea Sway got stuck. Would-be internationals can take heart from the fact that Lucinda was eventually eliminated after two falls.

During Lucinda's last half-term holiday from school, she saw an advertisement in the *Horse and Hound* for the sole progeny of Sheila Willcox's Fair and Square. As Fair and Square had won at the Burghley Three Day Event that autumn (1968) she automatically assumed he would be a brilliant event horse.

Be Fair was then five years old and she first saw him with her mother in the stables of Hagley Hall in Worcestershire. Lean, with a ribby body, clipped pale-yellowish chestnut coat, Be Fair had a scar around his near fore from one side to the other behind the heel, where he had been caught in wire. Both Lucinda and her mother rode him and Lucinda bravely and happily jumped the railing into the park without mishap. Lady Doreen decided to buy him subject to a veterinary inspection.

November 7, 1968, was Lucinda's fifteenth birthday. She was back at St. Mary's School, Wantage, having regretfully assumed her mother had not bought Be Fair because she had not heard anything. Then a greetings telegram arrived with the words: "Many Happy Returns Darling, Mummy, Daddy, Be Fair." Lucinda remembers, "At last, I had a proper horse of my own and felt very important."

But horses are great levelers. On her first ride on him at home, he continually spooked and refused to pass any unexpected piece of paper or leaf caught in the wind unless given a lead. He would rear up with the balance of a circus horse onto his hind legs and whip around very sharply.

Her father, who had been in Australia when Be Fair had been found and purchased, wanted to see the family's new acquisition in action. The horse demonstrated a shattering ability to nap and rear at any obstacle he did not relish, and even fell over backward. Lucinda was sickeningly aware that having her first "proper" horse also meant she had a king-sized problem on her hands.

Even as a fifteen-year-old, the resolve that has helped make Lucinda one of the world's top event riders was apparent and a plan of campaign for Be Fair's further education was evolved and carried out.

A season's hunting with the Pytchley in Northamptonshire with a very experienced farmer, Tom Payne, proved an inspired move. Three day event trainer Dick Stilwell, who had helped with Sea Sway, was a continual adviser in the further education of both Lucinda and Be Fair.

After a series of one-day horse trial outings the pair was finally on the route to stardom when they caught the eye of the Junior Three Day Event Chef d'Equipe, the late Colonel "Babe" Moseley. Lucinda and Be Fair were members of the British Junior team which won the 1971 European Junior Championships at Wesel in West Germany. Lucinda was placed eleventh overall.

Later she competed at Punchestown, the premier Irish three day event, finishing fourth at her first attempt at a senior three day event. Lady Hugh Russell and Mrs. Pat Burgess both gave her immense help at this time.

On Lucinda's first appearance at Badminton in 1972 she finished a commendable fifth, improving to win in 1973. This victory earned her a place in the British team for the European Championship in Kiev in the Ukraine in 1973. There she soared over the difficult second cross-country fence which had annihilated so many hopes, but after a courageous approach was unfortunate to fall at the relatively simple sixth fence. This was in a wood and Be Fair was probably unsighted by a trick of light through the trees. Be Fair is so athletic and like a cat that this seemed the only explanation as he banked the fence and somersaulted. Nevertheless, she remounted and finished twelfth overall.

A fall at Badminton in 1974 lost her a chance of a team place, but she was chosen as an individual for the World Championships at Burghley. There she made the costly error of going too slow on the steeplechase course while the United States and U.S. rider, Bruce Davidson on Irish Cap, powered home to the team and individual gold medals.

The following year, with her mistakes behind her, Lucinda lost no time on the complicated figure-eight steeplechase course at the European Championships at Luhmühlen on Luneburg Heath (scene of some of the fiercest battles of World War II). Closely attended by her father and mother, she went on to win her first European Championship and to lead Britain's first, highly controversial all girl team to the European silver medals.

The subsequent fall she won the Dutch Three Day Event at Boekelo on Wideawake, the horse who so tragically collapsed and died at Badminton in 1976 after carrying her to her second victory there.

Be Fair then slipped his Achilles tendon off his hock after clearing the final fence at the Olympic Games when Lucinda and Britain were in sight of Olympic medals. Although he happily recovered sufficiently to compete at a few minor trials and is the "king" of the Appleshaw yard, his days as an international horse were lamentably over.

In 1977, Lucinda accepted the ride on Mrs. Hugh Straker's brave George, a horse which Captain Mark Phillips had earlier partnered and with which he sustained the occasional fall.

The new combination never looked back; they captured Badminton (where Lucinda was also third on Charles Cyzser's Killaire), and led Britain to the team championship at Burghley where Lucinda deservedly retained her European Individual Title.

1978 proved a testing year. She decided she did not wish to subject George to further international events. Captain Phillips then took over the ride, but subsequently agreed with her and George was retired, still a valiant hero.

Lucinda then rode the temperamental but brilliant Irish horse, Village Gossip, into second place at Badminton behind Jane Holderness-Roddam and Warrior.

Gossip, brilliant although occasionally chancy across country, is a demanding dressage prospect and at this stage although not achieving total communication with Lucinda, responded relatively well to her superbly tactful riding.

After her father's death in the early autumn of 1977, Lucinda found herself without her main adviser and much loved staunch supporter. Financially, she found she would be unable to carry on, but a plea for financial support on television brought forward concrete help from the container ship company, O.C.L. Overseas Containers Limited, which made it realistically possible for her to continue.

Lucinda's vital personality and enquiring mind have contributed to making her continually seek for and achieve improvement in a self-assessive quest for perfection.

For years she has been buying young horses. She starts by looking below her prospective purchase's knees. "If I don't like the look of that I don't look any further because it's absolutely not worth it for eventing. I've learnt that even if a horse is otherwise perfect, if it's back at the knee, leave it. I like to have a horse with a touch of hunter blood, a touch more sanity and less nervous reaction than many thoroughbreds. Basically, I prefer short backs and it helps now if you have a little ex-

Major-General Erroll Prior-Palmer watches his daughter Lucinda giving her international partner Be Fair a kiss.
PHOTO: LESLIE LANE

travagant movement. Across country I like a short striding horse like Village Gossip, who never lengthens his stride and gallops the same way because you can be so much quicker on them. He is the fastest horse I have ever ridden and you can get round every corner just like that – bang. I'd almost rather leave a great raking stride; you spend a lot of time crossing fences on that type of stride. Natural rhythm and free movement are two of my priorities and if you can find a horse with a nice temperament it is a help.

"Looking back, I realize that Be Fair and I were both adolescent when we first met and when I think of all the terrible things I did to him when I was learning, like putting him into fences upside down, I thank God for his marvelous sense of self-preservation." Be Fair was fifteen years old in 1978, but still enjoys the occasional day's hunting and hunter trials.

Lucinda is the only British rider to employ the international training method, interval training, that Jack Le Goff introduced so effectively to the United States Equestrian Team (winners of the 1974 World and 1976 Olympic Gold Medals). He had become interested in the system when he saw it practiced by athletes in France. It is impossible to write down the exact formula because it depends on the type of horse, terrain and type of competition in view.

The American rider, Bruce Davidson, alerted Lucinda's attention before Badminton, 1974, by laughing at "the way the English riders galloped through the woods for hours on end," and then went on to win the World Title at Burghley. "I laughed back at him for laughing at us and worrying about heart and respiration, but soon realized that what he said made sense, because it has always been my ambition to get my horses fit with the minimum of effort and keep them sound. I liked the way the American horses continued to look big and never looked like rats."

Lucinda first tried interval training after Badminton, 1974, and finds, "It brings on the horses by leaps and bounds." The work is being continually broken, but going for longer periods. The principle of interval training is that the second effort comes just before full recovery from the first. If the first work day on this system was a working canter at 15 m.p.h. for three minutes, a two minute break and final three minute canter, the effort demanded by the second canter uses the horse's body far more progressively, increasing the horse's capacity and thus fitness. Each rider usually has his or her own special variation of the standard four-day work plan with day one a rest day building up to day four, the highest work point.

Looking ahead Lucinda says, "Olympics to me are not the be all and end all. My main challenge is to learn to ride and to be a master of three facets, not a jack-of-all-trades. Nevertheless, there would be something special about winning although often Olympics don't produce the best people whereas most internationals do. The Montreal Olympics were an exception, they produced a really true result. I think Tad Coffin, the winner, is brilliant and the Americans are the best."

She is undoubtedly very competitive; "I could not face the continual slog of training were it not for the actual excitement of competing. I just love making youngsters, riding horses round courses and the feeling of satisfaction when they are going well."

Few young riders have broken through to the top since Lucinda – a fact that has not escaped her. "I have recently become aware of what we lack by way of mental approach, facilities and money, to go and get the right type of instruction.

"Most riders of eighteen are just as I was and would rather give up riding than spend time on the end of a lunge line getting a correct basic seat. I would like to have an influence on the need for clinics for young riders, feeling it important to make up riders' minds early on; not to teach, but to give a few talks." One such clinic was held at Lord and Lady Hugh Russell's Wylye House in Wiltshire in summer 1978, with Lucinda having a chance to give the sort of advice she advocates.

"I think that, if the sport alters, it will be increasingly like a pentathlon with a higher standard of dressage, a more difficult steeplechase course – the cross-country doesn't need altering – but bigger show jumps. At the moment you can win without being particularly good. With fewer roads and tracks this would also make it more of a spectator sport and encourage sponsors. The sport has been like it is now since 1928 and, although many people won't agree with me, I think it is time for a change."

With her quick mind, attractive looks and *joie de vivre*, Lucinda has been a very definite asset to three day eventing in the 1970s. She constantly analyzes her performances, not only when she falls off, but when she is successful: "If I win I could usually have gone better. One of my very few ideal rides was in the 1975 European Championships at Luhmühlen on Be Fair." Wherever she goes from here, she will certainly be onward bound.

Robyn Smith

Jockey

ACCORDING TO THE Daily Racing Form, by September 4, 1978, Robyn Smith had ridden 2,410 races. She had won 238 times, been placed second 242 and third on 261 occasions. Her total purse money was $2,570,562.

While equestriennes have proved the equal and often the better of men in show-jumping, horse trials and dressage contests, partially because they often establish a special bond and sympathy with the horses they ride, the race track proves an entirely different challenge.

There is no sport that requires a tougher professional approach. Riding a horse in a big crowded field, avoiding the many pitfalls that can cause a nasty fall when trying to find an opening for a strong run from the back, or holding an exhausted horse together to win by a head in a desperate tough finish make the very highest demands on both mind and body.

Jockeys need lightning reflexes and the utmost degree of coordination. Most have to diet constantly and watch the scales because their desirability disappears as soon as they become overweight. Continual early morning starts, out on the track at Aqueduct or Belmont at 5.30 a.m. each day, as the traffic streams the other way into New York, and early nights to maintain their energy and make it all possible, allow only the very minimum of socializing.

For a girl to become a jockey in this relentless world, which until the 1960s was totally dominated by men, is a very formidable project. Racing is not only a sport but a very demanding big business, not concerned with excuses but about winning.

Crouched over Santa Fe's mane is jockey Robyn Smith at Belmont Park, New York. WIDE WORLD PHOTOS

The men who organize racing are basically psychologically opposed to girls and there are few bettors who would not prefer to put their money on a horse with a male jockey.

A number of female jockeys have come onto the scene since Barbara Jo Rubin achieved the distinction of being the first girl to win a race at New York in March, 1969, but although many showed ability, most departed, lacking the utter determination necessary to fight for the rides on which to prove themselves in the callous and ruthless racing world.

Robyn is, as she says herself, "a very private person."

She was born in Hawaii thirty years ago, attended college in California, where she majored in English, and then briefly became a film starlet and attended acting school at Columbia. She had always loved horses as a child, but because of an allergy which later proved to be to hay and dust, not horses, did not begin to ride until late. Soon she was skipping acting classes rather more than she was attending them in order to have more time to ride.

At about this time, she met Bruce Hedley who trained at Santa Monica, begged him to let her ride exercise and, after much persistence, was given the chance on some headstrong two-year-olds, learning as she rode. Although she often experienced some difficulty getting them back to the stables, she always succeeded in doing so.

When she heard that Kathy Kusner had been granted a jockey's license in Maryland, she applied for one at Santa Anita, but not surprisingly was turned down, because at this stage she lacked experience.

Eventually, with the combined backing of trainer Jerry Dutton and the Kjellquale Stable, the Golden Gate Race Track granted Robyn a license and the next step was the California County Fair circuit. This entailed a series of one-night stops in grubby motels and constant travel, but she also won her first race on the Ferndale half-mile track. It was, however, a tough place to further her chosen target, getting to the top as a jockey. The last girl at the fairs, Anna Lee Mills, had also ridden Brahma bulls at rodeos.

By now, Betty Jo Rubin was regularly riding in New York. Robyn decided she wanted to test and prove herself by riding on the best tracks in the United States.

She arrived at Belmont at the worst possible time, just as the track was shutting down for winter and most of the stables setting off for Florida. She went knocking from barn to barn at Belmont but no one was enthusiastic about offering a ride to an unknown girl jockey until finally trainer Frank Wright took pity on her and took her on contract as an apprentice or "bug" rider.

When she came back to New York in 1972 with much more experience under her belt, the Argentinian trainer Horatio Luro gave her a ride at Aqueduct in the mud and she edged home by a nose. Allen Jerkens, trainer for the very successful Hobeau Farm Stable, was one of the first to realize she was better than the average apprentice and his perspicacity resulted in her winning on three of the first five horses he gave her to ride.

Gradually, life seemed a little less tough. Occasional appearances in the winner's circle were the best advertisement for her talents, and most important, she gained the reputation of being one of the few apprentice jockeys for whom horses really ran, and also of being a good worker.

One definite asset at this stage was her appearance. She is fine-boned and lithe, five feet, seven inches tall and slim and fit from tennis, golf, fishing and cycling, as well as riding horses, weighing around one hundred and two pounds. Had she so wished she would have had little problem establishing herself as a successful model. Now she is frequently seen in television commercials, but at that time she was really struggling to establish herself and get rides. Soon after her arrival in New York, the attention she drew from a wide press who waxed lyrical with such phrases as "Her face would fit a Grecian coin," may have irritated her, but the burst of attendant publicity and overexposure at that time served her well, because the mass of features and articles meant that everyone involved in racing was at least aware of her endeavors and ambition to become a top class rider. And owners and trainers naturally assessed her ability.

One owner whose attention she caught was Alfred Gwynne Vanderbilt, and she has since ridden some good horses and won on them for the Vanderbilt stable.

Her good looks are not always helpful. Certain owners and trainers do not use her as a jockey because she is slim, attractive and articulate; their wives are said to forbid them to engage her to ride. Robyn, who needs all the good rides she can get, must find this exceedingly hard to take.

Going backstage at the New York tracks, one realizes that there is an excellent rapport between the regular jockeys which is both helpful and heartening. One piece of good fortune came her way when Dick Mead, who had been valet to top jockeys Eddie Arcaro and John L. Rotz, came forward and offered his services when it was announced that she was to ride in New York. All the other valets groaned disapprovingly.

In the "Big Apple," jockeys, regardless of sex, quickly fade from the limelight if they do not have what it takes. The moment of truth when many apprentices disappear is when they lose their last so-called "bug" and trainers can no longer claim the final five pounds allowance when putting them up. At this stage, although she did get the chance to ride less frequently, she still got some useful good horses, especially from Jerkens, and with continual wins, a critical stage in her career was passed.

Even though her opportunities are definitely restricted, she has succeeded in figuring among the top riders in the averages issued daily by the New York Racing Association.

Robyn is hyperactive and thrives on the trips she is now assigned out of town at such tracks as Liberty Bell on the outskirts of Philadelphia and Delaware Park outside Wilmington, Delaware.

The experts are unanimous that she has improved beyond recognition since she first rode at New York in 1972, which is not surprising as her initial rides were comparatively late in her life. Among the people who have commented on her progress are: Cordero who said, "She has improved more than anyone I see"; Rotz, "I never thought she would do anything like this and I told her so. Of course Robyn never pays any attention to you when you tell her a thing like that"; Chuck Baltazar, "I'd say determination is one of her strongest points, she never gives up"; Laddy Adams, "Robyn has some 'smarts' about her, namely she is very alert, intelligent and cool during a race." Trainer Jerkens, who has taught her a great deal of what she knows, handed her a king-size compliment when he said, "I never saw her lose a race she should have won."

Robyn Smith walks to the paddock with Angel Cordero Jr. before a race at Belmont Park, New York. WIDE WORLD PHOTOS

To a degree, Robyn has patterned herself on Arcaro and studied his book, *The Art of Race Riding*, which was how she really mastered in detail the difficult art of how to switch a stick. Pushing a horse toward the finish, weight well forward, hands of silk, strong legs and head buried in her horse's mane, she bears much resemblance to the master.

Robyn Smith's success is partially due to her ability to establish a quick understanding and trust with horses; this has nothing to do with her sex but is a gift given to some of both sexes. Her consuming love of horses and the rich pattern of life around the race track has been another helpful factor. Her fellow jockeys have unquestionably appreciated her determination. They speak of her with warmth and once they are down at the starting gate, no favors are asked and certainly none given for the duration of the race.

The greatest praise was unspoken and it should surely please Robyn Smith that no one I spoke to said: "For a girl she rides really well."

Christine Stückelberger

Dressage Champion

SWITZERLAND'S CHRISTINE STÜCKELBERGER was by no means the first lady ever to win an Olympic Dressage medal when she became the individual champion with Granat at Bromont in Canada in 1976. Denmark's Liz Hartel, although limited by a severe attack of polio, became the first to win a medal in any equestrian discipline when, riding Jubilee, she was second to Major St. Cyr of Sweden in 1952 at Helsinki. At the following Olympics, held in 1956 at Stockholm, Major St. Cyr and Madame Hartel were again first and second, while Liselott Linsenhoff of Germany was third with Adular. Some sixteen years later, in 1972, on her own home ground at Munich, Madame Linsenhoff, riding Piaff, became the first lady to win the individual gold dressage medal. For good measure, the charming and seemingly effortless combination of Russia's Elena Petouchkova and her black Pepel was second.

Christine's victory was all the more impressive to watch because she is small and petite, in the utmost contrast to her partner Granat, a giant Holstein, with all the solidity and weight of his breed completely belying the enormous athletic ability and tremendous sustained power and extension of which he is capable.

Standing at ease in his stable, Granat appears to be a rather plain large brown gelding, but the exceptional level of training he has attained enables him to give a display in the dressage arena of superb gymnastic perfection.

Christine Stückelberger was born in Switzerland in 1944. Her grandfather was a former president, and her father, a

Christine Stückelberger and Granat on their way to victory in the 1976 Olympic Games at Bromont, Canada. PHOTO: LESLIE LANE

doctor. Her parents, who did not ride, lived in Berne. As a child she loved all animals and had her own fish, cats and dogs. She began to learn to ride and was soon in trouble at school for playing truant in order to spend time with horses, and collected some bad reports.

As Christine grew up, she became increasingly interested in riding and had lessons at the Berne Riding School where the Austrian trainer, Georg Wald, taught. He was promoted to the position of *Oberrichter* (leading rider) at the Spanish Riding School of Vienna in 1967. She soon developed a keen interest in dressage. As early as 1968, after only one year's specializing, she was the reserve rider for the Swiss Dressage Team at the Mexico Olympics with her first international dressage horse, Merry Boy. Wald is a world-class trainer but enjoys the stimulus of competitive riding which is, of course, not a part of the traditional activities of the Spanish Riding School. Consequently he resigned in 1971 to concentrate full time on training riders for competition.

When Wald moved to Salzburg to concentrate on teaching a few pupils who wanted to specialize in dressage, Christine went too, wishing to continue working with the same trainer. Then, when he set up a smaller establishment at Hobranz, in December 1975, on Lake Constance near Brag, just across the border into Austria, she also moved.

The fascination of watching Christine and Granat in action together derives from the great contrast in horse and rider together producing superb sustained movements. Granat stands 16 h.h. but appears larger by virtue of his substance, great muscular development and the way he uses himself to the maximum. Christine is five feet, four inches tall, fair-haired with gray-blue eyes and very light bones. The dissimilarity between horse and rider is so great that a newcomer could be excused for wondering whether the slight girl could control the powerful horse. Indeed, there have been occasions such as on a practice day at Bromont preparing for the Olympic Games, when Granat assumed charge and took off. He is so strong that it was some time before Christine could stop him.

World Dressage Championships, Goodwood, July, 1978. Colonel Sir Harry Llewellyn, President of the British Equestrian Federation, presents the F.E.I. Trophy to Switzerland's Christine Stückelberger, who has just won the title on Granat. PHOTO: FINDLAY DAVIDSON

Now, Wald concentrates on training aspiring dressage riders from Switzerland and Austria and the teams of both countries. He has twenty boxes and a small riding school. His most famous pupil, Christine Stückelberger, devotes a large part of her time to riding and schooling horses. She spends all morning working and training her horses, and in the afternoons either deals with the paper work associated with running the establishment, such as progress reports or competition entries, or she may help with work on the ground in preparation for such movements as the piaffe.

In December, 1968, she came upon Granat by sheer chance. A stallion she had gone to buy proved to be too expensive but at the same time she saw Granat. Her immediate reaction was that he was very ugly. Although he had a reputation of being "a little bit crazy," noting his powerful limbs, she bought him straight away and very cheaply.

When Granat arrived back home, she soon realized that he was, "Not a little, but very crazy, and really far too strong for me, far more suitable for a big man." However she persevered with his training, and in 1971 in Salzburg she became aware that he was producing a very promising piaffe and might well prove to be an exceptional Grand Prix horse.

Now he is Olympic champion and the pair has also won the 1975 and 1977 European Championships, the 1970–77 Swiss Championships and 1974 Aachen Championships. The only major title that has eluded her since she reached the top is the 1974 World title. But here, the majority of judges placed her either first or equal first and it was solely on account of the harsh marking by just one of the jury that the German, Reiner Klimke, won.

Granat's greatest asset is his natural big rhythmic movement. His deceptively frail-looking rider directs this so well into cadenced work that his hoofs barely seem to make contact with the surface of the arena. Christine finds his strength so great that it requires a big effort to sit in the trot and she is sometimes almost unable to breathe.

The huge Holsteiner is quiet and tractable in the stable, but outside, one problem is retaining his cool, because on occasion he can become a different horse from one second to the next if he sees or hears something that disturbs him. Clapping often upsets him and this can easily happen at a show like Aachen where show-jumping and driving contests are often run at the same time as the dressage competitions and the dressage arena is well within earshot of the main arena.

*1972. A rare moment of relaxation for Swiss dressage star,
Christine Stückelberger.* PHOTO: FINDLAY DAVIDSON

Christine does not worry whether her fellow competitors are men or women, feeling there are equal opportunities for either in dressage, providing both a good horse and a good teacher are available. But she does think that whereas a man can reach Grand Prix standard with a horse on his own, women do need the help of a trainer and would not be successful alone.

"Herr Wald, Granat and I are a team, we all three like to work together and get satisfaction from giving of our best. I can ride only with feeling."

Christine's battles with West Germany's Harry Boldt and Woycek were a feature of the 1976 Olympic and 1977 European Championships. When two riders and their horses are so close in competition on this high level, it gives them the necessary stimulus to continue to seek perfection in all movements and has made for a series of electrifying contests.

Possessing relentless determination and composure, Christine and Granat, a horse whom many dressage experts would have passed over as potential Olympic material, have provided enthusiasts of the 1970s with some of the most exciting moments ever in international dressage.

Then, eight and a half years after the triumverate of rider, horse and talented trainer began to work together, a moment supreme in Canada at the 1976 Olympic Games came when, with Granat's fabulous movement flowing to its maximum, Christine captured the ultimate prize of the dressage world.

In July 1978, at Goodwood in Sussex, she attained the elusive dressage triple crown when she won the World Individual Championship with Granat.

Helen Crabtree

American Saddle Horse Trainer

THE AMERICAN SADDLE HORSE DIVISION is a scene all of its own and there is no better place to see saddle horses than at the New York International Horse Show which is held at Madison Square Garden each November in combination with the American National Horse Show.

The horses which contest the three- and five-gaited classes are representative of a true American breed – the American saddle horse. The breed was established in the early 1900s and is largely a combination of standard-bred horses, thorough-breds and the Narragansett Pacer.

Gradually the breed was improved by the selection of first-class foundation sires in the state of Kentucky, which is the capital of the world of the American saddle horse. The saddle horse has arrived at its present stage through careful breeding by those who wanted to provide quality for people of a certain affluence. There has been no more successful rider or trainer of these horses since the turn of the century than Mrs. Helen Crabtree.

Mrs. Crabtree was born in Illinois with, as she describes it, "A dream, a compulsion for horses." Even when young she had childish fantasies about horses and never on any account wanted to be a nurse or automobile driver, which were popular future occupations in the nurseries of that time.

When only four years old she began to ride and one of her earliest recollections is of the farmers buying wild, incorrigible horses at the county fair in Morgan County, then gradually gentling them and getting their confidence – initially through

1965. Helen Crabtree was awarded "Horsewoman of the Year" by the American Horse Show Association. She is seen here holding the winning "students" Peacock Peavine ridden by Raredi Stuart who won the same award five years later. FOTORITE

grooming. While the other little girls she knew ate candy and went to parties, the young Helen avidly watched the local horsemen and learned early that the best way to train an animal is by conditioned response.

"Quite soon I had a chance to ride a borrowed spotted pony and had to do so in my little skirt. I saw a beautiful black pony ridden by a girl in a delicate pink organza dress, and while I was really envious of the pony, I thought the girl's dress looked just crazy. My childhood memories have colored my own teaching."

35

Now, whereas many saddle horse competitors appear in flashy sequinned riding clothes, Mrs. Crabtree and her pupils are always quietly elegant in well-cut clothes complementary to the color of the horse they are riding.

By the time she was fourteen years old, she had seized the chance to ride "everything on four legs," and already begun to do a little professional training. After receiving a B.A. at Illinois College in Jacksonville where she was an art major, she taught horsemanship there at MacMurray College, and later, during World War II, ran the Missouri Stables in St. Louis. In 1975 she received an Honorary Doctorate from Jacksonville.

Possessing enormous determination, Mrs. Crabtree has always been fascinated by logic, considering that if anyone wants anything badly enough, they can accomplish it, as she did when she decided she wanted to master and understand the art of riding. By way of an example of her desire to succeed, when she saw a photograph of herself on her pleasure horse at the age of eleven, she cried because it was so far from how she had hoped she looked at that time.

She regards horsemanship as an art form and tremendously cerebral, requiring 90 percent brains and 10 percent muscle. On entering what had until then been exclusively a man's field, she didn't feel threatened. "I also didn't realize that after I had carved the way, there would be others following. I have experienced no male chauvinism but have to admit that although I have won the World's Junior Championship for four-year-olds and under at Louisville, I think it would be very hard to win the World Five-Gaited Championship there because as a rule there are three men judging. I would like to be able to prove that I am wrong."

In 1956, when she and her husband decided to buy a property they quite naturally looked in Kentucky and settled in the verdantly green tree-dotted country of Shelby County. They have built up a saddle horse enterprise at Simpsonville with three farms combined together on 175 acres where they run a combined breeding establishment and training and teaching center. Riders taught by Helen Crabtree are con-

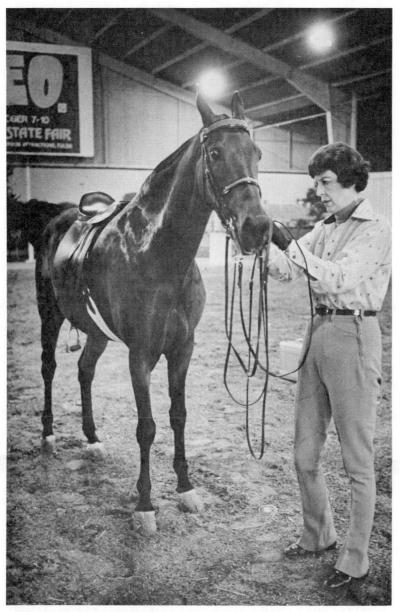

Helen Crabtree preparing Flamenco, World Championship winner in 1975, 1976 and 1977, for a work-out.

sistent winners of the major classes throughout Kentucky and at the National Horse Show.

There are now approximately 250 horses at Crabtree Farms Incorporated, which has developed into a complex self-sufficient enterprise which she runs with her husband, her son Redd, who won the World Grand Championship, and six other trainers.

The saddle horse is judged on performance, animation and way of going, conformation, quality and manners. The horse it most resembles in Great Britain is a large hackney as both have the same high head carriage and attain great elevation with their limbs – but there the similarity ends. There are two divisions of saddle horses, three-gaited and five-gaited.

The three-gaited horse is shown with its mane clipped and the upper part of its tail clipped or shaved. It is judged on its performance and the three basic gaits: the walk which must be true and flat-footed; the trot which should be balanced, collected and graceful with high animated action in front and behind; and the canter which must be smooth and easy.

The five-gaited horse is shown with a full flowing mane and tail and judged on the same three basic gaits with the addition of two more – the slow gait and the rack. The slow gait is a four-beat diagonal gait originating in the rear. Helen Crabtree elaborates: "The motor is in the rear and the forequarters are elevated by weight, as the rider moves back in the saddle, the hocks move well forward. It is a movement bordering on the levade. If well done, there should be a slight hesitation at the top which is most attractive."

The rack is a progression of the slow gait, a four-beat movement in which the hoofs strike the ground at regular intervals at speed with no hesitation.

Saddle horse producers are often criticized for the training devices they use, such as weights and restricting "action chains," but Helen Crabtree makes no use of these. She waits until she finds a horse with the right natural movement. These horses, she reasons, need much patience with their schooling to reach the high standard required to win in the show ring today, and will do better with inherent ability. One way you can separate the good from the bad trainers is that they are wise enough not to rush their horses with time-saving devices. The basic need is natural movement, which can then be enhanced by developing the elevating muscles.

"For me the beauty of a saddle horse and the essential loftiness applies to all elements and movements. The horse should have a short back, long sloping shoulders and long high neck to complement his motion. The best horses are bred to produce a strong drive from their hocks, their balance is slightly to the rear and to my mind there is much compatibility between good dressage and saddle horses.

"The unique factor about producing saddle horses for the ring is that they have to compete for at least forty minutes in a class but must demonstrate a high, seemingly effortless ground-consuming stride and action with sharp pricked ears, looking as natural as though turned out in the field for an hour. Ideally, they should look wild and free but contained with intermittent control on the mouth. Attaining this look demands tremendous endurance from the horses. They must carry far more fat than a runner and be trained to such a high level of obedience that if I racked into a wall, my horse would hit it if I didn't say 'whoa' at the last minute. Basically the horse is not free when being ridden but utterly dependent on the rider so that it can enjoy performing the different movements. It is an experience both happy and exciting to sit on a free moving fast saddle horse which displays complete tractability while giving the appearance of utter abandon."

The World Saddle Horse Championships are held concurrently with the Kentucky State Fair each August. Helen Crabtree has won an astonishing total of fifty-one World Championships.

Her philosophy is never to be insular or limited in one's own horizons by retaining a parochial view. "No matter how experienced a rider may be, he has always something to learn. Good riding knows no bounds and the top class rider should always be ready to make a minor adaptation or innovation."

The Queen Mother

National Hunt Owner

THE STORY OF Queen Elizabeth's entry and continuing participation in National Hunt racing is that of the resurgence of interest in the sport to which she has contributed so much.

Whereas King George VI was always very enthusiastic about flat racing with (like his daughter the present Queen) a special knowledge about breeding which has helped the Royal Studs at Sandringham, Wolferton and Hampton Court to flourish, Queen Elizabeth had for some time been considering the possibility of owning a jumper. She had always owned horses, although she had not continued the riding she learned as a young girl at the turn of the century.

Lord Mildmay, champion amateur jockey in the 1937–38 season and from 1946 to 1950, who so unexpectedly died in 1950, was the person who fired her with enthusiasm. One year when he was staying at Windsor Castle for a Royal Ascot Meeting, the seeds were finally sown and Queen Elizabeth embarked on what was to prove a great and exciting adventure.

Monaveen, an Irish-bred steeplechaser by Landscape Hill, who had been bought out of Ireland by his former owner the greyhound trainer Mr. Dal Hawkesley for a mere £35, was the horse selected. At the time Monaveen, then an eight-year-old, was trained at Epsom by Peter Thrale. That season he had won three steeplechases, and been twice placed, from only eight starts, as well as showing well in the National before jockey Tony Grantham came off when he made a mistake at the nineteenth fence.

Queen Elizabeth decided to share the horse with her

Epsom, 1977. The Queen Mother in the winners' enclosure greeting the Queen's horse, Dunfermline, winner of the Oaks. Leaning forward to address the Queen Mother is the Queen's trainer Dick Hern. PHOTO: J. MACNEE

daughter, Princess Elizabeth. A deal was completed for £1,000 which, it was to be proved, could hardly have been better spent.

Queen Anne had been the last Queen to have a runner, when on July 31, 1714, Star won a race at Ascot, which she founded, and which carried a first prize of £14. His owner, who had been suffering ill health for some time, died the following morning.

Monaveen's first race carrying the royal colors was at the genial rural setting of the Sussex racecourse, Fontwell. Princess

Elizabeth came to see the horse run and, still ridden by local rider Tony Grantham and carrying the top weight, he ran out the winner of the Chichester Handicap Chase by fifteen lengths from Random Knight.

The new owners could not have made a more auspicious start. This was the prelude to a further eight wins. These included a gallant try in the 1950 Grand National, when only seven of the forty-nine starters were to finish.

Monaveen led for the first circuit but made a fearsome mistake at the fourteenth – a plain fence. He had knocked the stuffing out of himself, but somehow kept on going and ran into fifth place behind the favorite, Freebooter, ridden by J. Power.

As always, Queen Elizabeth's first thought was one of relief that her horse was all right. There had been thirty-four fallers in the race. One of them, Royal Mount, had broken a leg and had to be destroyed. After a race she never leaves the racecourse until she knows that her horses are all right. When she is back home at Clarence House she nearly always telephones her trainer to make sure that her horses have settled after the excitement of the race, and have eaten up their evening feed.

The following May, Lord Mildmay traveled west for a weekend at Mothecombe, his Devon estate, where he failed to return from his customary early morning swim. There seems little doubt that the cramp which occasionally paralyzed him on the racecourse had struck while he was swimming, and sent one of the bravest, most popular and most honorable riders in the history of the sport to a premature death.

Only the previous month this cramp had deprived him of a race at Ludlow when riding his immensely promising new French horse Manicou. Seemingly set for a comfortable win, as he came into the last fence his head dropped forward and he was suddenly powerless. As the horse swerved to the left he threw himself off in violent pain.

Monaveen won a total of eleven races for his royal owners before his career ended in tragedy. When trying to win them a second Queen Elizabeth Chase at Hurst Park, he fell at the water jump, broke a leg and had to be destroyed. It was a sad day for all concerned. Many female owners have abandoned the sport after such a loss, but Manicou was to come to the rescue.

Manicou was by far the best of Lord Mildmay's young horses. He had won four flat races in a row for his trainer Francois Mathet in France before his career in England began, and had won two novice hurdles and four successive novice chases, which included the highly rated Broadway Chase at Cheltenham, a top three-mile novice chase.

Although he was a stallion he had a likeable character and was very robust, so in the summer of 1950 Peter Cazalet advised the Queen Mother to buy him. Cazalet trained at Fairlawne, near Tonbridge in Kent and had been in the same house with Lord Mildmay at Eton.

She was his sole owner. Her own colors of blue, buff stripes, blue sleeves, black cap and gold tassel had their first outing in the three-mile Wimbledon Handicap Chase at Kempton, when Manicou, ridden by Tony Grantham, made his owner the first queen to win a race under her own colors since Queen Anne. In doing this, after half a century, she brought back the colors of her grandfather, the Earl of Strathmore.

In December, many experts thought Peter Cazalet's entry of Manicou, then only a five-year-old, in the King George VI Chase at Kempton – which is not a handicap – over optimistic.

As Tony Grantham had not recovered from his fall when Monaveen sustained fatal injuries, Irish jockey Bryan Marshall was offered, and accepted the ride, and rode the horse to a splendid victory. Queen Elizabeth had driven down specially from Sandringham on icy roads for the occasion, and it had proved well worthwhile to see Manicou's greatest victory. The field included Lord Bicester's Silver Fame, winner of the 1951 Cheltenham Gold Cup, in which Manicou was sixth out of six runners. The only note of sadness was that Lord Mildmay was not there to share it.

By the early autumn of 1951 there was some bad news of Manicou, who had injured a leg and was out for the season.

But Peter Cazalet had heard of a promising Irish horse, Devon Loch, owned by Colonel Stephen Hill-Dillon who lived near Navan, and soon a fine strong five-year-old by Devonian out of a mare by Loch Lomond, by all accounts a real chasing type with a bold honest head, crossed the channel and arrived at Fairlawne.

He had won an Irish "bumper" race at Naas, and now ran well in three hurdles but without victory. After Christmas he was switched to fences. On January 17, at Hurst Park, he finished second, only four lengths behind the brilliant Mont Tremblant who was to win the Gold Cup just two months later, and so yet again it was evident that Queen Elizabeth had made an exceptional purchase.

All too soon she was to experience the vicissitudes of the sport. In his first and only race the following season, Devon Loch injured a tendon in a foreleg which necessitated firing. Peter Cazalet, aware that he had a well above average horse, was quite prepared to wait while rest restored the leg to full efficiency.

Shortly after Devon Loch's show of promise, King George VI died in his sleep in the early hours of February 6. He had, it seemed, been convalescing well after his lung operation in the previous fall, and had been enjoying a little shooting and the quiet country life at Sandringham.

For the following two years, Queen Elizabeth's racing interests were curtailed. Devon Loch and Manicou were both recovering from their injuries, but quite naturally she would not have wished to race until a considerable period of time had elapsed after the King's death.

It was apparent that, although she was taking no active part, Queen Elizabeth's enthusiasm for steeplechasing had in no way diminished when she drove to Cheltenham on a misty day in 1953 and saw the Gold Cup won for Ireland by Knock Hard, who was ridden by Tim Molony.

With Devon Loch still sidelined, Peter Cazalet purchased another French-bred horse. This time it was a strong seven-year-old bay gelding M'as-tu-vu. In his first three races the following season, he ran in Peter Cazalet's colors and was ridden by Dick Francis, who had earlier ridden for Lord Bicester and trainers Frank and Ken Cundell. Francis then replaced Bryan Marshall as the Fairlawne stable jockey. Queen Elizabeth bought M'as-tu-vu after his third outing, which was at Fontwell, when he won the $3\frac{1}{4}$ mile Whitelaw Challenge Cup.

Meanwhile, after almost two seasons' rest, Devon Loch was ready to go into training again, so in fall 1955 Peter Cazalet worked out a plan with the 1956 Grand National as the target. Devon Loch, who won twice before Christmas, was then held up in his work by deep snows in Kent; but although not completely fit, he raised his owners' hopes by staying on strongly and finishing third in the National Hunt Handicap Chase at Cheltenham.

With ideal weather and no television there was a big crowd at Aintree in late March. The royal party who traveled north with high hopes to support Devon Loch included the Queen Mother (as she had now become), her daughters Queen Elizabeth and Princess Margaret, and the Princess Royal.

The field of twenty-eight starters was smaller than usual, but included two previous winners, Early Mist and Royal Tan. Also running were M'as-tu-vu and Sundew, who had won in 1957. Dick Francis knew he must give Devon Loch time to settle and the horse jumped so well throughout that by the Canal Turn on the second circuit he was close behind Armorial III with his horse still full of running and the horses around him already under pressure. Clearing the final fence in fine style, Devon Loch landed in front to a tumultuous storm of cheering with Dave Dick, who was now the closest challenger on E.S.B., having virtually conceded victory, dropping his hands.

Only fifty yards from the post, Devon Loch's hind legs seemed to slip away from under him and he staggered and fell, but he did not roll over. Throughout the incident, Dick Francis remained in the saddle and somehow, with great difficulty, the horse struggled to his feet. E.S.B. now passed him on his way

Ascot, 1976. After winning the Fernbank Hurdle, Sunyboy receives a warm welcome from his owner, the Queen Mother. On the right is trainer Fulke Walwyn. PHOTO: HUGH ROUTLEDGE

to victory and it seemed that if Devon Loch could continue again he would be second, but he could not immediately propel himself forward with his hind legs. Francis now dismounted and Gentle Moya passed on the way to second place, followed some ten lengths behind by Royal Tan.

Devon Loch's ears had been pricked throughout. Subsequent tests did not reveal the cause of the fall. It has never been established whether it was a momentary heart failure, sudden attack of cramp, ghost jump, or the stunning effect of the sudden thunderous wave of sound as the crowd prepared to welcome home a Royal horse.

Queen Elizabeth bore her desperate disappointment with her customary courage, as with a smile she congratulated the winning owner Mrs. Leonard Carver. Both she and the

Queen were bewildered and upset as she tried to console a desolate Dick Francis and Peter Cazalet and gave Devon Loch, who quickly recovered, a pat with the words: "You dear, poor old boy."

Far from lessening her enthusiasm, this wretched experience seemed to heighten her determination to succeed. Soon she gave Peter Cazalet orders to buy her more jumpers and throughout the years she has had many good and brave horses carrying her colors.

Queen Elizabeth does not just follow jumping, but whenever possible is there living the occasion – and not only from her box. No matter how vile the weather, she is down in the paddock to wish her horses and riders well beforehand and see them back when they have finished to congratulate or console.

From 1956 onward, when Queen Elizabeth had three horses in training, they gradually increased. In 1959 there were nine, in 1965, nineteen, and by 1967, twenty-two. In the early times there had been about twelve runners in a season, but in 1966 there were over one hundred.

In the latter 1950s, her horses were found largely in Ireland by Colonel Stephen Hill-Dillon, who had found Devon Loch. They included Double Star, a nice little horse who was full of quality and won a total of seventeen races. 1960–61 was a very successful season with Gay Record, a $2\frac{1}{2}$–3 mile chaser, The Rip, a fine big horse with a club foot who was a special favorite, Jaipur and Silver Dome all winning races.

Peter Cazalet's favorite stamping grounds were Lingfield, Sandown, Fontwell, Plumpton, Kempton and Hurst Park. His horses usually produced their best form here earlier in the year than Cheltenham. At the London park courses he was a tremendous force. These courses were also convenient for their owner to pay frequent visits to watch her horses race.

In both the 1961–62 and 1964–65 seasons, she won more races than any other owner. In the 1961–62 season with ten horses in training she won twenty-four races and £9,208.5s. stake money and the French-bred Laffy won the Ulster Harp

National. In the 1964–65 season with nineteen horses in training she won twenty-seven races and £13,158.6s. stake money.

This was the era of Gay Record who ran the large number of twenty-five times for his royal owner. There was also Worcran, a big lop-eared chestnut who was later used at Windsor as a hack by her daughter, the Queen, and the exceptionally handsome dapple gray, Chaou II, who had a real star personality and won seventeen races. He was French-bred and a most competent three-mile chaser.

There were, of course, the losses that are almost inevitable to any steeplechase owner. Escalus died in the late 1960s of colic after winning hurdles in brilliant style.

More recently there was Game Spirit who had proved her most prolific winner with twenty-one races to his credit. A beautiful and honest chestnut, he was at his best at $2\frac{1}{2}$ miles on ground that was not too soft. He was a superb jumper who never fell and finished third in the Cheltenham Gold Cup. His final year was to prove a sad one. After running a tremendous race when beating Bula at Newbury, he was then last of three in the King George VI Steeplechase at Kempton on Boxing Day. He was very restless afterward and was given an electrocardiograph to check if anything was wrong, but when it revealed nothing, he was given a long rest.

His final race was a $2\frac{1}{2}$-mile chase at Newbury in 1977. He was a real gentleman and jumped superbly but, giving away pounds of weight, was passed before the post to finish fourth. On his way to the unsaddling enclosure, he dropped dead and a post mortem at the Bristol Veterinary College revealed a massive hemorrhage of the lungs, probably caused by the hard race with Bula. He had lived up to the name, Game Spirit, in every possible way and his death left an enormous hole in the stable as he was a great character and splendid horse.

It must have been a great shock for Queen Elizabeth, but when she was told, quite typically, her first reaction was to comfort her jockey, Bill Smith, and trainer, Fulke Walwyn, who had taken over this role when Peter Cazalet died in 1973.

Over the years, several jockeys have ridden Queen Elizabeth's horses, first Tony Grantham and then Bryan Marshall, Dick Francis, Arthur Freeman, Bill Rees, Richard Dennard, David Mould and now Bill Smith. David Mould summed up all their feelings when he said, "She is the most wonderful lady. I was fortunate enough to ride for her in eighteen of my twenty years in racing. She is so interested in everyone connected with the sport right down to the lowliest lads. Whenever I was in hospital, she always sent me books to read. She has a special love of her horses and was very proud of the fact that she found The Rip herself, grazing in a field behind a pub in Norfolk. Makaldar, a wonderful dark chestnut, who was bred in France and won fifteen races, largely over hurdles, and Game Spirit were certainly two of her favorites. She never leaves a racecourse without first being sure her horses are all right."

For the 1978–79 season, Queen Elizabeth's horses in training are likely to include Colonial Lad, a five-year-old chestnut gelding sired by Sir Winston Churchill's stallion Colonist when he was twenty-seven years old; Tammuz, first class over hurdles, but plagued by leg trouble and Queen's College, a very bright prospect who is by the stallion College Green, teaser at the Royal Stud at Wolferton. A deep-set chestnut, College Green stands little over 15 h.h.

Queen's College, like Isle of Man, is by Manicou out of Queen of the Isle, and is home-bred, as were Inch Arran and Colonius who were also out of Queen of the Isle.

Recently, Queen Elizabeth has turned her attention to breeding steeplechasers as well as buying, a project that demands patience, but which is both interesting and rewarding. And so her visits now include not only early morning trips, well wrapped up in raincoat, sou'wester and gum boots, to see her horses at exercise, but visits to Sandringham where she keeps her brood mares. Her horses also enjoy their summer rest there under the watchful eye of her daughter's stud manager, Michael Oswald.

Queen Elizabeth now has a few brood mares which she visits

whenever possible at Sandringham and some youngsters at Hampton Court.

Her genuine interest in her horses is never more clearly demonstrated than when a horse has finished its racing career or – she is rightly professional in outlook – if it is not up to the job at hand. They are not sold at random but, with total disregard for financial gain, placed in good homes. For example, the gray Inch Arran, who so often featured on televised races in the early 1970s, for some years after his retirement continued to enjoy life to the full as a hunter with Ian Farquhar, Master of the Bicester.

Queen Elizabeth reads and studies form with great diligence and has become very knowledgeable. Like other steeplechase owners, she takes the *Racing Calendar* and *Sporting Life* and an exchange telegraph system has been installed at Clarence House so that she can listen to a commentary of the races in which her horses are running. She keeps in close touch with her trainer, Fulke Walwyn, and they frequently have talks on the telephone about the horses in training at Saxon House, Lambourn.

Queen Elizabeth now probably derives as much pleasure from seeing one of her babies win, especially if it is a home-bred one, as anything. When she first entered the multi-colored tapestry that is English steeplechasing after World War II, she was regarded with a degree of awe as a royal owner in a sport which was then a mere shadow of the crowd-pulling and well-sponsored draw it has recently become. However, it is no exaggeration to say that she is now a much loved integral member of the complicated scene which she adorns so well.

Cynthia Haydon

Driver of Hackneys

UNIQUE, I HAVE ALWAYS understood, is a word that should be used sparingly. In this book, I have chosen to use it to describe Cynthia Haydon's eminence in the driving world where she has been without peer for over three decades. That is a record which makes Lester Piggott's or Pat Smythe's splendid achievements pall in comparison.

It is beyond doubt that Mrs. Haydon is the best whip alive today, a star in her own right, and half of a remarkable partnership, with Frank, her husband of close on forty years, that has bred and produced hackneys that are, quite simply, the best available since World War II.

In 1974, the Hurstwood Stud, which comprised about seventy horses at the time, moved from Shovelstrode Farmhouse, near East Grinstead in Sussex, to Manor Farm on the edge of picturesque Lower Slaughter, a stone village two miles south of Stow-on-the-Wold in Gloucestershire, where it now operates as the Cotswold Stud.

On a bleak January day with huge snow flakes whipping past the windows through which tourists peer in summer, it is warm and comfortable sitting by the huge open fire. The house dates back to the fourteenth century in parts and has been beautifully restored to the original by Frank Haydon who is something of a specialist having done this on two previous occasions.

The star of the driving arenas wherever she competes, from the Royal Winter Fair in Toronto to the elegance of the Royal Windsor Horse Show, is wrestling with a giant elm log – which

*Mrs. Cynthia Haydon driving her team of hackneys at the 1976
World Driving Championships at Frauenfeld, Switzerland.*
PHOTO: FINDLAY DAVIDSON

must measure five feet long. Its positioning to give maximum heat is proving far more of a problem than driving a four-in-hand of fractious hackneys. When Mrs. Haydon speaks, it is with a warmth, welcome and flamboyance that makes one feel instantly at home.

She sits down with the inevitable twinkle in her eye, tell-tale of a king-sized sense of humor, and her famous cigarette holder jutting out of her mouth. She is staunch and gray-haired with the rosy complexion of those who, regardless of the weather, are daily to be found outside working their horses.

Her husband Frank, whom she married in 1939 when aged only twenty, lowers his six feet six inches into the chair beside her and gives her an indulgent smile. One of a series of multi-buttoned telephones flashed behind him; as administrator and organizer (he has been dubbed the impresario to the star), he runs the stud and large staff with a jet age efficiency more akin to that expected in a high-powered specialist factory.

Mrs. Haydon's astonishing reign at the top of the driving world began with her birth because her father, Robert Black, was a leading light in the hackney world. He had gradually progressed south from Dumfries, via Yorkshire to Reading where he established and owned Maiden Erlegh Stud, showing the inmates with considerable success both before and immediately after the war.

The young girl Cynthia, however, was not instantly enamored of hackneys. Her initiation came early. "When I was about five years old, if my uncle was going to take out a quiet horse, he'd put me on his knee and toddle off for a drive. I showed kids' ponies from ten to sixteen years old and wasn't at all keen on driving at first. But, you know how things fall into place. Although I didn't want to drive at the time, one day I pinched a hackney pony from my father in York and did the lot, rode, drove and showed it, and found it all fun.

"I was at boarding school at the time and when I left, my father had started a riding school for me to run at Maiden Erlegh. My mother wanted me to go to a domestic science college but that didn't appeal at all so I went to help my father.

But, at that time, it was a seven-day-a-week job and I didn't enjoy it. It was not so much the fact that I had to buy my clothes out of my half-a-crown a week wages, but the utter boredom of taking out two rides daily over the same route.

"Then in 1936, the late Bertram Mills, who founded the famous circus and was a leading driving authority and exhibitor, sent down four hackney ponies and four Welsh-hackney crosses for two teams. My father was short staffed so I fiddled about with them. One day Bertram Mills came down to see them and as there was no one else about, I pulled them out for him and he said, 'That's just the girl I want. I will teach her.'" This was to prove the launching of the reigning queen of the driving scene.

"I was frightened to death of him," she recalled, "but he taught me the art of driving, and after my seventh lesson, I was considered ready to take his team to the International Horse Show in 1936 when it was still held at Olympia. When those huge doors flew open, I was so terrified I dropped all four reins but Frank here was there to help me." She finished third with a hackney pony four-in-hand and has not stopped winning since. "I continued to drive for him until the war loomed up, when he died and all his hackneys were sold."

In 1939, luxuries such as driving hackney horses and ponies came to a temporary halt, and, when war was declared, Cynthia Haydon, who was just married and living at Sleeches Farm near High Hurstwood, Sussex, was entrusted with the care of two brood mares, Erlegh Maiden and Gloria Mundi. These, her husband, now Private Frank Haydon of the Royal Fusiliers and R.A.S.C., had just bought. Today, some of the Haydons' best hackneys are descended from these two foundation mares. At the end of the war, part of which had been spent in India and Ceylon, Frank returned home with the rank of Lieutenant-Colonel. His father, who lived in Carshalton, Surrey, had a chain of butchers' shops and bred hackneys as a hobby. When he died in 1934, Frank kept a few horses but sent them to Robert Black to produce at shows.

At the onset of war, Robert Black and his wife sold their

Maiden Erlegh Stud and went to live with their daughter. In 1956, Frank decided to sell out his butchers' shops because he realized that the new business which was quickly developing at Sleeches Farm had great possibilities. The time was opportune, and they were not afraid of hard work. There was a revival of interest in hackneys and Robert Black, his daughter and son-in-law had a nucleus of top class horses, suitable premises, the essential know how, and business acumen.

With these assets, the success of the enterprise was assured, and it was not long before their business had developed into the position it holds today as the foremost hackney establishment where people from all over the world go when they want information about the training and showing of hackneys or to purchase winning material.

After founding the Hurstwood Hackney Stud, so named because Sleeches Farm was at Hurstwood, the Haydons realized that Sleeches was no longer large enough and were able to buy Shovelstrode Stud Farm near East Grinstead. The previous owner was the late Mr. J. A. Dewar who had kept such well-known thoroughbred stallions as Cameronian and Fair Trial at stud. Robert Black now decided to retire.

At Shovelstrode there were 255 acres, farm buildings, many of which they converted into supplementary boxes, and a well-constructed yard of brick boxes. Private tarmac roads which linked various parts of the farm provided first-class areas for driving young horses, away from the busy Tunbridge Wells–East Grinstead road, which was suicide alley.

The Hackney Horse Society of Great Britain was founded in 1883 but the hackney horse was in use long before then. It was found that as early as 1259 in some old records of English farm accounts which Norman invaders brought with them, fast trotting horses were called "Hacquenees," a French derivation from the Latin word "equus," meaning horse. In 1266, one of these Hacquenees was sold for 200 shillings and in 1286 it doubled to 400 shillings, but dropped to 20 shillings by 1330.

In 1340, a law was passed that Hacquenees were to be kept only for the King's men and officers and not to be used for farm work. Henry VII and Henry VIII insisted that the stock of England be improved and increased, and made great efforts to do so. It is certain that the ancestry of the hackney on the sire's side is founded on a similar basis to that of the thoroughbred and traces back to the Darley Arabian. He was a genuine Arab, bred in the Desert of Palmyra and considered to be of remarkable beauty. He took his name from Richard Darley of York who imported him in 1704 as a four-year-old.

In the heyday of the age of horse transport, the hackney was regarded as the equivalent of the Rolls Royce of carriage horses. With their courage, high action and effervescent good looks, they were the choice of the *beau monde* for driving.

The most distinctive characteristic is the fierce ground-covering knee action with the foreleg being thrown well forward rather than just up and down. The action of the hind legs is the same but to a lesser degree. "They should," Cynthia Haydon says, "appear like ballet dancers, hardly touching the ground as they tread over it."

Ideally the hackney's personality and performance are both brilliant and his action correct and true. His head should be small, neat and intelligent with large bold eyes and small ears. His body should be compact with great depth of chest, his shoulders powerful, withers low, his legs short with good bone and his tail held high.

He is of outstanding versatility and stamina, being admirable for private driving and combined driving competitions as well as an ideal carriage horse for a park drag. Hackneys are exceptional show horses because their speed, rhythm, animation and exciting high action never fail to catch the eye of the public.

From the end of the last war to the late 1970s, Cynthia Haydon has been in a class of her own in the hackney show world. From 1946–1977 at the National Hackney Show, the Haydons have shown and produced the Supreme Champion Harness Horse on twenty-seven occasions and the Supreme Champion Harness Pony on twenty-nine occasions; also the Supreme Harness Horse or Pony at the Royal International Horse Show on thirty occasions.

Mrs. Cynthia Haydon silhouetted in the Wembley arena.
PHOTO: FINDLAY DAVIDSON

Hurstwood Superlative, who was foaled in 1949, is singled out by the Haydons as the best of their stream of champions. Standing 15.1 h.h., her dam was Erlegh Maiden and her sire Solitude. "Every foal Erlegh Maiden produced was a champion bar one who died. Nearly all champions in any country in the world go back to Solitude. He came to us with a bad reputation of not being able to bridle, but then pre-war trainers couldn't get a horse to bridle. You have to be a bit of a psychiatrist to train and show hackneys. Superlative was brilliant but very temperamental. I never knew until I was

57

actually in the ring if she was going to give a dazzling or a wretched performance. I never carried a whip with her because she could hear a flea squeak, let alone wind in a whip. I have never seen an animal with so much action. She may not have been the very best of lookers but was the most sensational going hackney in the history of the breed."

Multi-winner Brookacres Light Mist, a descendant of Gloria Mundi, wins the accolade for being the easiest to drive. "Right now, we have a bunch of two-year-olds to break and it's really fun. I think we have both come to enjoy the training even more than the showing. When we were in our thirties we were on the road all the time. Now we only aim for the major shows, Royal Windsor, the South of England, which incorporates the Hackney Horse Show, the Royal Show, the Royal International Horse Show and the Horse of the Year Show."

Until recently, Mrs. Haydon used to show once a year in the United States at Devon County in Pennsylvania and once in Canada at Toronto at the Royal Winter Fair. At both shows she drove for the top American exhibitor, Chauncey Stillman of Wetherfield, New York. His main interest was breeding hackneys for pleasure rather than showing them and the main object of his showing was to stimulate interest in the breed. At Devon County one year, the ring was suddenly flooded after heavy rain. The competitors were ready to enter, hoping the class would be canceled and they would avoid a soaking. Then Cynthia Haydon drove into the ring, her horses and carriage immaculate, and splashed through the water to win the class. One suspects that Mrs. Haydon must have allowed herself a smile as she received the winning rosettes and the band, displaying great presence of mind, broke into "Britannia Rules the Waves."

Mr. and Mrs. John McDougald are the Haydons' leading Canadian clients. They own the hackney four-in-hand which Cynthia Haydon shows with great success and also stand a thoroughbred horse, Idiots Delight, at the Cotswold Stud.

But then, "Devon became too much of an effort, it was a great rush as it usually comes immediately after Windsor. For the last two years, 1976 and 1977, we've made just one journey a year across the Atlantic to Toronto where I judged the coaching class. It is well supported and in 1977 there were twelve four-in-hands and a mixture of breeds such as Morgans, standard-breds, Holsteins and Gelderlanders."

As professionals, the Haydons sell high class hackneys all over the world. Some of the countries who regularly purchase are the United States, Canada, South Africa, Mexico, the Argentine, Costa Rica, Australia, Holland, Italy, Portugal, Spain and Japan. Hardly surprisingly, the Haydons do not advertise and often the horses are bought unseen and leave for their new owners without veterinary certificates. "We naturally stand by every horse that we sell. With the economic depression in Great Britain, the best customers are now overseas and well into five figures is not impossible for an exceptional animal."

The carriage house contains fourteen vehicles painted dark green and black, superbly maintained and kept under canvas covers. Among them stands a coach by Holland and Holland and phaetons and gigs by Lawtons and Mills. It is hard to assess their ever-spiralling value but when a private four-in-hand drag that had been leased from Bernard Mills was sold at Reading Market in 1975, it made £15,000 ($31,000). "The old carriages outstrip the new ones by a long way and it is far better to buy an old one and have it done up," Mrs. Haydon volunteered. "Pre-war brass furniture on both carriages and harness is generally of far better quality. Although harness makers today are few and far between, more are getting involved because it is an up-and-coming sport, especially with the combined driving competitions and British Driving Society classes."

One long wall is completely hung with gleaming well-maintained sets of harness. "All we have has been handed down and is either sold or reconditioned." It includes the late Bertram Mills' brass monogrammed four-in-hand harness.

In a separate harness room are kept all the breaking tackle, headcollars and articles in daily use. It is in this inner sanctum that Cynthia Haydon enjoys spending time mending any harness other than that used for showing, which is sent away.

"When our circus moves town, we usually take two horse boxes with a specially designed trailer carrying our show vehicles behind each one and the land rover pulling the caravan." Bearing in mind the cost of transport, the fact that a set of four-in-hand harness might well cost $8,000 (£4,000), that a potential top class hackney would be unlikely to cost less than that, and the additional cost of grooms and maintenance, it is interesting that in 1977, Jubilee Year, there were eighty-five exhibitors at the National Hackney Show whereas in 1952 the number was sixty.

That hackneys are experiencing a revival of popularity in Great Britain is to a very large part due to the Haydons' long-standing showing and breeding success. The advent of the F.E.I. combined driving competition provided a further challenge to Mrs. Haydon and in 1972, at Munster in Germany, with Mr. Douglas Nicholson and Sir John Miller, she was a member of the British team which won the first-ever World Championship to be held. Typically, she gained more satisfaction from the fact that her team of hackneys proved their intelligence, stamina and versatility by completing the dressage test, cross-country marathon of well over twenty miles and final intricate course of obstacles in a restricted arena, than the fact that she is still the only female competitor ever to have competed in an international F.E.I. competition with a four-in-hand.

She has now given up combined driving, probably not as she said when she won the 1977 Martini Driving Award, "Because I am getting too long in the tooth," but because of increasing back trouble. During the 1970s she was badly kicked by Florescent and "knackered for a season." Subsequent visits to a specialist revealed that some discs in her back were worn out. As she now experiences more or less continual pain, bumping along over a long demanding marathon course cannot be fun and she says, "I just wish that combined driving had begun fifteen years ago."

The world's greatest lady whip, Mrs. Cynthia Haydon.
PHOTO: MONTY

Now she probably experiences most pleasure breaking and training the youngsters, which takes place when the horses are two years old. Her eyes gleam with pleasure as she shows me the horses that are currently being worked. "The Playpen," a round arena fenced in by strong wire mesh, is where the horses are lunged prior to being put into breaking carts. "The horse must know who is boss," she says, "but unnecessary roughness gets you nowhere. What you must have is patience. Most people are in far too much of a hurry. Just occasionally you may have to put a horse on his nose so he understands once and for all who is in charge." The young ones are all driven in long reins because this helps develop balance and matures neck, forearm and quarter muscles which produce the distinctive hackney action.

There are a few fortunate pupils at the stud who come to drive, not as working pupils, such as American Mrs. Sidney Smith who is a regular visitor. "There is far more to driving than riding a horse and much more to their training. The first vital stage is putting the harness on the right way. That takes about ten minutes. The set of the blinkers, 'winkers,' is important, but it is even more essential to have a noseband in the right position. This helps the sit of the entire bridle and no horse will be happy if it is pinching."

As in all spheres of the equestrian world it is now sadly a rarity to find judges with practical experience, such as horse veterinarian Howard Dawes in the hackney world who regularly drove himself while working as a junior partner in Sheffield. As the number of judges with such experience decreases and in view of the increased international interest, judges now often come from abroad, particularly from Holland.

"A show horse must never have a chance to lose his brilliance through getting stale," Frank Haydon emphasized. "To avoid this the experienced stallions receive a lot of work in long reins rather than being driven and the coach horses are often ridden out into the country to break the monotony."

When Cynthia Haydon appears in an indoor arena at night in London and the house lights dim, remember that the sturdy determined figure in control is in no way as forbidding as she may appear. Wearing her already legendary well-tailored brown suit and the inevitable brown felt hat ("never outshine the horse," as she says), she is more than likely to play a practical joke on a fellow exhibitor during a display. But make no mistake, this woman of innate kindness is beyond dispute one of the world's most talented whips ever, possessing a combination of superb hands, sensitivity, character and knowledge. She is an undisputed master of her art and the Haydons' eminence in their field will, in all probability, never be equaled.

Alison Oliver

Horse Trial Trainer

IN OCTOBER 1976 ONE OF the leading three day event trainers, Alison Oliver, moved from the very successful establishment she had set up at Warfield, in Berkshire, to Churchill, near Chipping Norton in Oxfordshire. Her aim was to continue training riders for horse trials, for which she had established a considerable reputation, but on a smaller scale than previously so that she could devote more time to bringing up her two young sons, Philip and Christopher.

Alison Coulton spent her childhood in the village of Aughton in Lancashire. Her parents were not interested in horses but, like many other pony mad children, their daughter was soon saving up all her money in order to spend her free time at the local riding school, which was then run by Harry Monks and is now the Northern School of Equitation. Alison joined the local pony club and eventually her parents bought her a pony of her own.

By the time she left school, Alison was sure she wanted a career with horses and went to work for a nearby farmer's wife, Mrs. Hilary Booth, mother of Hazel Booth who won the Midland Bank Championship of 1970 on Deemster and the important Midland Bank International Open Section of Wylye Horse Trials on Monacle II in 1977.

Alison, who had by now already ridden in some pony club events, persuaded Mrs. Booth, who had a show pony and a show hack, to try eventing. Gradually, Mrs. Booth became interested in horse trials.

This provided a first-class start for Alison because Mrs.

Booth had a real feeling and understanding of horses and would often help her when she worked the horses. They both shared the same attitude to horses and knew what they hoped to attain from each one. It is extremely important at this stage of an equestrian career to have a sympathetic owner and Alison was fortunate in her employer; their joint enthusiasm often kept them talking late into the night.

When Alison heard that international dressage rider Mrs. Gold wanted someone to help her in her stables at Warfield she went there for a month and it was agreed she could watch the top dressage horses working.

At this time, Mrs. Gold was working her dressage horses Gay Gordon and Roman Holiday. The Swedish trainer, Lars Sederholm, was already taking some lessons there and when the month was over it was arranged that Alison would stay on. Soon both she and Lars began taking in a few horses for training.

They worked together a great deal and proved complementary to each other. Alison had the experience of having competed at such major three day events as Badminton and Harewood and a number of one day horse trials and so knew about getting the horses fit and what the practical side of eventing involved. The fact that Lars had spent some time working for the outstanding Swedish international horseman and double Olympic gold medal dressage winner, Major Henri St. Cyr, meant that Lars already had a relatively advanced knowledge of dressage. This was an enormous help and Alison's second lucky break. Both were deeply interested in horses and their development, and most of their spare time was spent discussing their charges and how best to obtain results and overcome problems.

Eventually Lars left to establish the Waterstock Training Centre near Oxford and Alison took on the business for Mrs. Gold. She also married Alan Oliver, an international show jumper, who has now achieved the same standing as a course builder.

The Warfield establishment proved very much a full time job with twenty-six boxes, a riding school and thirty-six acres

*Burghley, 1977. Alison Oliver congratulates Lucinda Prior-Palmer
on her second European Championship victory.*
PHOTO: FINDLAY DAVIDSON

which were invariably in full use. Mrs. Gold gave Alison
complete responsibility, which proved invaluable, and at first
Alison continued to compete. In 1966 when she was thirty she
received an accolade when she was invited to ride Foxdor by
the Combined Training Committee, finishing twelfth on him
in the World Championships at Burghley. During this period
she also took in horses for training and helped their owners.

In 1967 Alison had a third lucky break when Princess Anne
came to her for training. At this time Mrs. Gold was District
Commissioner to the Garth and South Berkshire Pony Club
of which Princess Anne was a member and through the

65

Crown Equerry, Colonel Sir John Miller, it was eventually arranged that the Princess and her horses would receive their introduction to eventing from Alison.

At first Alison competed on Purple Star, Princes Anne's first event horse, and later Doublet, but eventually she found that competing, training and attending events with the Princess was too much and she gave up her own competing. At about this time, David Hunt, now a professional dressage trainer in his own right, came to train as a working pupil under Alison.

Alison found Princess Anne marvelous to work with because "She has an understanding and natural feeling for horses. I often think girls are more sensitive than men about the horses they handle. When I explained to her a certain horse's character, and how I thought he should be worked, she quickly understood what I meant."

It was unavoidable that the Princess was often away on official duties at a vital stage during some aspects of her horses' training. This disadvantage was overcome by Princess Anne's ability to pick up the critical stage of their work and so progress was very quickly made.

Together trainer and rider gradually established a superb partnership which flourished with Doublet. He was the horse which carried the Princess to the 1971 European Individual Championship at Burghley. Alison assessed him as "A most honest genuine horse, who loved his work and put into it his all. Soon after he arrived, I realized that he had ability. My only doubt was that he might be highly strung and a little temperamental; after we had worked him for a while one would never have believed that he could have been difficult."

The strength of the partnership was emphasized in the way that, despite the Princess having to be rushed unexpectedly to the hospital and missing crucial stages of Doublet's pre-championship build-up, she quickly attained the very high standard, both physically and mentally, that was necessary to win.

Alison's move from Warfield occurred for a variety of reasons. Warfield was near the steadily developing Bracknell New Town, and the area was becoming very built up. She had a wonderful period there, but with heavy traffic it had become less suitable as a venue for training horses. The property belonged to Mrs. Gold and Alison had now been there for eighteen years. While both were keen and agreeable to forming a partnership, it became apparent to Alison that if she was ever to move that this was the most suitable time. Her husband, Alan, now had no show-jumpers, as his top international partners had grown old and been retired. The Warfield establishment had grown rather larger than Alison really required.

She envisaged a smaller and rather different menage. She now had people who wanted to come with their horses, look after them and receive tuition. With fewer horses to ride, she would not have to hurry through a day, losing the genuine enjoyment she experiences in training and teaching people. She still has one very good helper, and working pupils and clients, so quite a number of people can have their horses trained there. There are seventeen acres, an indoor school, and up to eighteen horses can be accommodated.

Jonathan McIrvine, 1977 Tidworth winner of the City Section on Mr. J. Martin's Magnus, who was training there in 1978, helps with much of the riding and teaching. He plans to devote his life to horses. About this time, pupils include Suzanne Collins and her event horse, Watertight, who is concentrating on dressage, seventeen-year-old Maureen Piggott (daughter of Lester Piggott), and another promising young rider, David Morrison.

Local riders also bring their horses for lessons and Alan gives experienced help with the show-jumping, especially in the winter. This is an additional benefit to Alison's pupils.

Most years, Alison goes to the United States and regularly helps Pip Finch, who has a sizeable private enterprise at Southern Pines, North Carolina.

Alison's success is structured on her basic philosophy. She considers that winning in three day eventing is based on a bold cross-country horse, with an athleticism about him.

If she gets a new horse into the stable, she likes to ride him to find how he reacts to a rider on his back. Nearly always she finds that they react adversely to something, the most obvious being the rider's legs on his sides or the rider's hands, or the rider's seat. In the first instance, the horse must accept happily that there is a human being on his back with hands and legs to control him. In rather a passive way, she tries to relax the horse so that he is completely at home carrying the rider.

"A horse nearly always puts you in the position of the rider who rode him before, because riders normally accommodate to their horses. When he is not resisting, or ignoring hand or leg, but is accepting that the rider has contact with him, and letting him sit comfortably in the saddle, then you can start influencing him.

"The next move is to start balancing the horse over his own four legs. Some horses instinctively run away from the leg, but it is very important that they do not." Alison is very careful not to take away a horse's personality or the enjoyment from his work if he disobeys. When he understands what is wanted, a moment arises when she takes him to task and puts him in order. She is prepared for this moment of truth in order to maintain mutual respect. She keeps the work very varied in order to maintain the horse's attention.

Alison's philosophy is to study each horse individually and never to generalize about their training. One reason why she prefers working with only a few horses is that it is easier to arrange an individual work program for each horse, to establish and maintain the essential and very special rapport between horse and rider.

Part of her success results from teaching young riders how to understand why a horse is doing something wrong. "There is nearly always a reason for this and however difficult the horse is, I always remember that there is always someone, somewhere who can find an answer to the problem. There is invariably a key to the situation somewhere. Understanding the psychology of the horse and rider you are training and how to bring the best out of them is very important.

"Every day, I realize more and more that it is horses who are the trainers. You can find that something works on one horse,

Alison Oliver. PHOTO: FINDLAY DAVIDSON

try it out on another and get results; and then try it on a third without success. Then comes a test when you have to try something new."

She enjoys working with difficult and sensitive horses and Chris Collins' brilliant Irish bred horse Smokey VI, who was a member of the British team that won the 1977 European Championships, is certainly in this category. When Lars Sederholm was ill in 1977, Chris Collins came to Alison as his friend and trainer with the same basic principles for help with his ever-problematical dressage on this horse.

Alison's approach to such horses is to analyze their difficulties and what they are reacting against. She tries to be passive so that they accept that she is there, and then she gradually approaches and influences them, after she has realized their problem.

"Chris allowed me to ride Smokey and I worked him a little and influenced him to a certain extent. I made him relax to me. Then I gradually helped Chris on him. I think I slowed Chris down, as he was riding the horse far too daringly and quickly. I watched him ride a test and he was hurrying from one movement to another. I advised him to give the horse time to do each movement and make him execute it correctly. In slowing Chris down and making him more correct, both he and Smokey had more time to complete one exercise, start the next, execute it and then begin to think about the next. He had been very much rushing through and this in itself had been exciting the horse. By asking for less, he got more relaxation and more suppleness."

At Burghley the help that Chris and Smokey had received from Alison really was beneficial. Smokey was far calmer and never looked like blowing up as he had on so many other occasions, and they finished a much improved seventh after the dressage.

It is fortunate that this talented trainer, who puts such emphasis on having her riders in mental and physical harmony with their horses, should be available to help the British three day event and dressage riders for many years to come.

Mrs. George Gibson

Judge and M. F. H.

IN 1975, MRS GEORGE GIBSON broke into what had hitherto
been exclusively man's domain when she became the first
woman ever to be invited by the Hunter Improvement
Society to judge at the Thoroughbred Stallion Show at Newmarket with the well-known trainer Jack Waugh as her co-
judge; already in 1969 and 1974 her great knowledge had been
further recognized when she was invited to judge the mares
and foals and then the young stock at the Hunters Improvement Show at Shrewsbury. She has also adjudicated at the
Royal Agricultural Show at Stoneleigh, Kenilworth.

Two incidents related to judging illustrate her great knowledge and enormous attention to detail. At the Hunter Improvement Show, one of the country's leading exhibitors of show
hunters had a gelding with a parrot mouth. (This is an irregu-
larity in which the teeth of the upper jaw project a considerable
extent beyond those of the lower jaw.) This is normally considered to be a bad fault in a show horse, as well as hereditary.
The mouth should theoretically be perfect in conformation,
and such horses are often bad doers as they have difficulty in
grazing and are sometimes oversensitive about the mouth.

Despite this flaw, at the leading shows throughout May and
June distinguished judges had continually put the horse among
the prize winners – a fact that had become quite a talking point
in the show hunter world.

The animal was an eye-catcher, and Mrs. Gibson duly
called it in in the first three of a large class. Inspecting the line
of horses more closely her hand moved to the horse's mouth.

She had a discreet word with the leader and in the final line-up the horse was placed right down the class. It was not noticeable at shows during the rest of the summer.

At the same show I was very fortunate to have a winner when my home-bred non-thoroughbred yearling Chandler headed his class. Three years later Richard Bowers, who had bought a half share in the horse, took him for a day's hunting with the Cottesmore for experience. By then Mrs. Gibson had become a joint Master, and amazingly, never having seen the horse in the interim period, she went across to Richard, took a closer look at Chandler, now 16.3 h.h. and well up to 14 stone 7 lbs., and said, "Isn't that my yearling winner from the 1974 Hunter Show?" A quite remarkable demonstration of knowledge and memory.

No one is born with the depth of knowledge that Mrs. Gibson possesses. It can only be acquired the hard way, through years of first-hand experience.

Joan Bradley was the eldest of a family of six, and as her father, Percy Bradley, was a farmer and dealer in the Cottesmore country where she has always lived, she had the ideal opportunity to learn about horses from her days as a very small child.

Her home at Barrow was only five miles from Oakham where she now lives. Her first pony was "a tiny weeny black-and-white Welsh Mountain pony mare called Maid of the Mountains that I distinctly remember riding for the first time with a frock on." They soon became regular partners, and the pony's winter duties included pulling her owner over the snow on a toboggan.

She soon progressed to the hunting field, where she was accompanied by her father. "I was brought up on hunting and was soon going out four days a week. At first I was terrified of jumping, but one day everything fell into place and it seemed easy. My father bought some lovely ponies from Horace Smith. We always rode out at 7 a.m. to do the shepherding. It was excellent schooling for horses and ponies. I showed them in the summer and hunted them all the season. They were always most beautifully clipped and trimmed. On the less fashionable days I usually went with my father, who would be schooling a young horse. There were no trailers or boxes in those days, and I remember well the excitement of setting out with him to hack to a distant meet as early as 8.30 a.m. and the joy of coming home together in the dusk after a good day, and people calling good-night as we rode through the villages."

Mr. Bradley had a reputation for finding and producing top class Leicestershire hunters to a very high standard, and as his daughter grew up and progressed from ponies, she had the fine experience of helping him and learning much from working with such quality material.

When she was sixteen her family moved to Chapel Farm, close to Oakham. There were sixteen stables, fields with a variety of fences to gallop over, and friends were always dropping in to give their point-to-pointers a gallop. "For me those were the halcyon days of hunting, the country was virtually all grass and you could just jump, jump, jump, with rarely a worry about wire. Even with about three hundred people out, one could ride over a wide area, take one's own line and really see hounds work, which is the great joy of the real foxhunter."

Horses were quickly bought and sold, and she soon learned how to adjust tackle for different horses, to check everything carefully before hunting, and to notice immediately if a horse was not one hundred percent fit. She also began to be able to advise her father which horse would be suitable for which client.

Over the years the Bradleys had been friendly with the Gibsons, the well-known veterinary surgeons who lived in Oakham. When George Gibson returned newly qualified from university he took over some of the Bradleys' veterinary work, with the result that when she was twenty-one years old Joan Bradley celebrated her birthday by getting married to George.

At first they lived in a small house in Oakham. Mrs. Gibson continued to hunt in winter and show in summer, and also had two sons, David and Michael. When George's father died they moved into their present home, Highfield, which, although in

Left, Mrs. George Gibson, Joint-Master of the Cottesmore heads the field

the center of Oakham, has a sizeable stable yard and paddocks behind it.

She had a number of good show horses, among them Burrough Hills, a 15.2 h.h. small hunter named after a famous cover, and Star Attraction, a liver chestnut hunter that showed well under both saddles and hunted brilliantly all the winter. There were also two home-bred horses, Wedding Rehearsal, who was almost unbeaten in brood mare classes, and Regal Mist, who was unbeaten in four-year-old classes and won a number of point-to-points and hunter chases. Mrs. Gibson also helped with the stallions as George was keen to continue the stud farm that his father had always maintained.

After the war there was a shortage of good horses for hunting, so in the early 1950s, in company with two close friends, "Migs" (The Hon. Mrs. Edward Greenall), and "Boodley" (the late Lady Helena Hilton-Green, later to become Lady Daresbury), and with advice from her father who was now in semi-retirement, she decided to set up a dealing business. The venture provided the high-spirited trio with endless fun. One day George suggested to Migs that she should clip and hog a horse that she had bought from a local person in a rough sort of condition and sell it back to him. To his delight she took up the challenge and went ahead, and sold the same horse back to the unsuspecting person. The whole thing was an even better joke as the buyer himself was always playing any sort of prank on his friends and this time Migs did the leg-pulling (though she later gave him back his check). They had countless trips to Ireland and many adventures. Once she rode and bought a nearly unbroken horse. Mrs. Gibson remembers: "In the veterinary yard at the Royal Dublin Show after riding the chestnut mare the oldish dealer said with a delightful smile, 'Well then – and I never expected to see a lady get up and ride a barely backed three-year-old.' Needless to say that was afterwards, not before. The horse was called 'The Wig.' This was because at Dublin he had the most lovely long full tail, but when he arrived in England he had a short rat's tail with hardly any long hairs. I wrote and protested and sure enough the beautiful false tail, a perfect match, was sent – and as the seller said, 'it was better to show him at Dublin with the tail *on*.' He was a marvelous horse and a super jumper." Eventually the trio were persuaded to end their dealing activities and thereafter concentrated once again on showing and hunting.

Happily both of Mrs. Gibson's sons took immediately to horses, and rode many point-to-point winners. David, the elder, was only two short of his hundredth winner when he had to give up because he was so badly smashed up. He now runs the family Barleythorpe Stud, and Michael is in the family veterinary practice as a horse specialist. It speaks much for Mrs. Gibson that she was able to say to me, "I have a marvelous collection of daughters-in-law and ex-daughters-in-law. They are all real friends and I feel very flattered that they bring their prospective husbands to me for my approval."

With all this experience and a very acute mind, it now seems almost inevitable that Mrs. Gibson would receive the accolade of becoming the first lady to judge at the Hunter Improvement Society's Thoroughbred Stallion Show. It proved, "An absorbing experience, moving into what had up till then been a man's world. There was so much to do; you are given the breeding beforehand to have time to study it carefully. I feel it is a priority to have a sound animal to produce sound stock. Basically I look for a big strong middleweight type with quality, the type I've been lucky enough to ride all my life. When a class comes into the ring I look first for presence – a nice air and a good walk. The horse must have scope, be deep and I love well set on limbs. I deplore the tendency these days to overlook weak hocks and curbs. If horses are to be genuine hunters they must use their hocks. It is a big strain jumping out of deep places and boggy rides can cause even more harm to hocks. He must have a sloping shoulder so he is a comfortable ride; even with a young horse I always visualize where the saddle will go. It is no good a horse looking a picture if he does not give the right ride. In that case I would always put up a plainer horse if it were an excellent ride."

A showman has to try to gild the goose into a swan. "I have

to assess the faults and weigh them against the good points which the good showman will have considerably glamorized. I remember one lovely pony whose stifle went in and out with a big clicking noise. It had won and continued to win a great many championships, but it was not sound and, despite the difficulties and embarrassments this caused, I had to put it out of the prizewinners. The degree of defect of spavins (a swelling on the hock) is sometimes difficult to decide. Bog spavins are not so bad; parrot mouths have no defense.

"I was lucky to be brought up in a dealer's yard, and of course when I was first asked to judge I thought I should put the world to rights. Very soon I made an awful gaffe. A well-known lady judge put my name forward to judge at a county show. I was eighteen years old and there were no judges' selection committees in those days. I was judging the hacks and thought they looked rather stale and much ridden in tight circles. The sixth was plain, but well shown and a heavenly ride. I moved it up to first, and immediately one of the stewards said, 'Someone in the stands say it's lame.' I was obviously overconfident, but as I had seen a message conveyed from the lady judge who had promoted me to the steward in the middle of the ring, I was incensed and it stayed top. It was as sound as a bell. That's one important point about judging. You must stand on your own feet and not listen to other people or stewards. It's your opinion that you have been asked for, and you must stick to it. My lady friend gave me a good 'dressing down' afterwards. I did apologize as she thought I'd let her down, but I said I would always much prefer to stick to my own opinion. A judge must be prepared to answer politely and with absolute assurance why he or she has placed an animal up or down in classes.

"In the Dublin Show one year I was requested by the committee to ride ponies in their classes. It was most interesting to ride a few of the 14.2 h.h. and 13.2 h.h. Most of them were delightful and beautifully balanced. It made the difference of one or two placings in each class. There is a tendency to judge too much on beauty and less on manners, mouth and ride

*Mrs. George Gibson, the first lady to be invited to judge at the
H.I.S. Stallion Show at Newmarket seen here with joint judge
Jack Waugh.* PHOTO: LESLIE LANE

sometimes. With a hunter I might overlook a small fault if he
really gallops. A horse with a small amount of knee action may
prove a more comfortable ride than a daisy cutter."

She considers it very hard for young judges to establish
themselves today because shows do not like putting up young
unknown judges. "Stewarding first is a good way to learn to
cope with the many situations that arise such as lameness,
wind problems, misbehavior and riders who come in when the
class is half judged."

Mrs. Gibson's prowess in judging has made her the re-
cipient of several invitations to judge abroad in Nairobi and
Johannesburg, where she found a very smart big permanent
building like an uncovered Wembley, but animals which were
mostly off the race track and sometimes unsound by English
standards. "I found I needed enormous elasticity in my

reasoning, but it was an extremely enjoyable experience."

Each show presents a different problem. She remembered her first time judging at the Hunter Improvement Show in the mares and foals ring. "I'll never forget the feeling, mares and foals, mares and foals, nose to tail. I really had to pull myself together to concentrate on the classes."

She is chairman of, and has carried out a great reorganization and standardization of the Working Hunter Pony classes and initiated the popular Nursery Stakes (ponies not exceeding 13 h.h.) and Cradle Stakes (ponies not exceeding 12 h.h. for young riders). This was a tremendous boost for the pony world as there is now an exceptional market for stronger ponies and ponies that grow over height for their respective classes. In 1976, 1977 and 1978 she was pleased to be asked to steward at the Fernie point-to-point, and in 1978 also filled this role at the Melton Hunt Club races.

A further accolade was her appointment in 1977 to be Chairman of the British Show Pony Council, as successor to the late Albert Deptford. This was the first time a woman had been appointed since Mrs. John Tilling and the late Brig. J. Allen founded the British Show Pony Society.

Mrs. Gibson has been closely involved with the Cottesmore Hunt all her life, never having lived more than two miles from the kennels at Aswell. In 1976 she became one of a triumvirate of Masters with good friends Mrs. Diana Hellyer and Mr. David Samworth.

When she was asked to become a Master in the spring of that year, Mrs. Gibson was in the hospital, "all jacked up," having sustained a bad fall out hunting when the horse she was riding came over backward on her. It did not belong to her and was suspicious of hounds. Mrs. Gibson's right leg was fractured in three places above, through and below the knee. "It was the best possible way to speed my recovery when I was told that as Master I should be ready to go cub hunting by August. I came off traction at the earliest possible moment and had concentrated massage.

"It was and is my job to buy all the hunt horses. My judging experience stood me in good stead. As we went round the dealers I had to balance on the car bonnet on my crutches and was able to say to the huntsman who was doing the riding, 'No, that rides short in front,' or 'I don't think that one will wear well for hard hunting work.' It is a matter of regret that I am unable to give more time to study hounds and their breeding, but one gets the utmost pleasure in watching hounds work out hunting."

As well as buying all the hunt horses she is entirely responsible for the stables, stud groom and staff, and visits them at least every other day. The Cottesmore Hunt has a very long and vivid history, and records indicate that it was first hunted in 1666 when Viscount Lowther brought down his hounds from Lowther in Westmorland. At the turn of the century his descendant, the Earl of Lonsborough, the famous "Yellow Earl," was Master of what had become established as one of Britain's most fashionable packs, and the current Masters maintain the hunt's proud tradition over a country which is now more ploughed than before.

She is responsible for the Monday and Thursday country and has to coordinate with all the farmers in the area likely to be hunted across, be sure that livestock such as sheep will not be disturbed, and arrange the drawing of coverts. These may well have to be altered on the morning if the wind is in the wrong direction for the draw. And when damage has been done or people disturbed, she must visit them either on the way back from hunting or that evening.

Going in as a lady Master presented no problems. As a farmer's daughter and hunt member all her life, she closely understands the problems of modern hunting, and receives the utmost cooperation from the farmers.

Princess Anne

Three Day Eventer

TO BE A PRINCESS in the world of horse trials is no sinecure. There is no more demanding challenge to any rider or horse than the three day event. To face this in the full glare of publicity with the world's reporters and photographers assembled to cover every move, whether brilliant or disastrous, is no advantage in a sport which sets the utmost tests of courage and concentration. Also, carrying out official duties means that vital training periods are often intermittent in a sphere where it is advantageous for horse and rider to school regularly together to build up a trusting partnership.

From an early age, Princess Anne clearly enjoyed the ponies she was given to ride. She progressed through riding with the Garth and West Norfolk Pony Clubs and as often as possible when away at school at Benenden, Kent.

Throughout the Princess's career in horse trials, her ability to establish a special sympathy and understanding with her horses stands out. This is particularly noticeable when she talks about Doublet and Goodwill, the horses on whom she has been most successful to date, and it is a bond without which progress in this highly competitive field is not possible.

Four years after her initial venture into horse trials, Princess Anne finished fifth at Badminton on Doublet in 1971. The event was won by Captain Mark Phillips on Great Ovation. He was later to become her husband. This placing assured her an invitation to ride for Great Britain in the European Championships as an individual the following September.

The mount that helped her to this breakthrough was

Doublet, by the Argentinian thoroughbred Doubtless II out of Swaté, who was also bred in Argentina and formerly in Prince Philip's string of polo ponies. As his breeding suggests, the chestnut gelding was originally intended to be a polo pony but when he grew to 16.2 h.h., Princess Anne, who had watched him growing up in the field, was given the chance to event him as it had become obvious he was too big for polo. Later, in 1970, the Queen gave Doublet to Princess Anne as a Christmas present.

At this stage, the Princess was learning about eventing and riding Purple Star with the help of trainer Alison Oliver who was based at Warfield, so very conveniently placed nearby. Doublet arrived when the Princess had been working with her trainer for a year. "Alison started Doublet and took him to one or two competitions at the end of the spring so I didn't get to know him properly until he had been there a while." The Princess found him very aloof in the stable; he used to stand and gaze out of the door and was generally stand-offish. For a long time she felt she was making no progress. Nevertheless, she won the first time she rode him in competition and so qualified for the Midland Bank Championships which were held at Chatsworth in 1969. Interestingly, it was the same year that Janet Hodgson and Larkspur, with whom she was to be on the British team in Luhmühlen (1975), also qualified.

After that, the Princess still thought that she would do more with Purple Star, so it was some time before Doublet came to the fore as a particular hope. Then the year the Royal Family went to Australia in the spring, Richard Walker, who had won Badminton in 1969 on Pasha, rode Doublet a few times. On her return, Princess Anne worked him for a period under the supervision of the Swedish trainer Lars Sederholm at Waterstock, near Oxford, because Alison was expecting her first baby. Suddenly the years of work began to pay off and her star was in the ascendant.

The fact that Princess Anne and Doublet were placed fifth in their first Badminton says much for their joint character and courage. "After that, I began to have a rather different impression of Doublet. I was so amazed by our progress that now I started to concentrate on him far more. I was still very green because the only other three day event I had ridden in was Tidworth with Purple Star.

"Looking back, it is a pity that as I was starting out myself, I failed to realize what a very good horse Doublet was. I now find this very sad in a way. He did not have the limitless scope of Goodwill and it was all done through his brain power and courage. Sometimes I wonder, if I had known more, if I could have taken better care of him and saved him. But quite certainly, he came to love his competitions so much that conceivably he would have made a terrible pensioner. He might have gone on and done reasonably good dressage, but I doubt that he had the physique for top class dressage. He adored the whole atmosphere; if there were more than a dozen people watching, he changed completely and did it all himself. He was a real showman, he did it because he wanted to show how good he was."

Doublet's high placing at Badminton had won the Princess the chance to compete as an individual for Great Britain in the European Championships at Burghley, but an emergency operation two months beforehand put her participation in jeopardy. There was no problem about Doublet, who continued his preparation in the capable hands of Alison Oliver. Rider, trainer and horse had now attained such a degree of understanding that the Princess would be able to ride at the last minute. The question was, could the Princess possibly be sufficiently fit to face the physical strain of a three day event so soon after being in the hospital and inevitably losing muscle tone?

At the time, the Princess considered her chances: "Fair in terms of finishing the competition. I had no real ambition beyond that. I thought I'd get fit enough in time and all along said that if anything hurt, I'd call it a day, so in that respect I was lucky. I trained as much as I could when convalescing in Scotland, running on the decks of *Britannia* and up and down the Scottish hills to this end. When I arrived at Burghley, I

Formative days. Princess Anne and Doublet at Chatsworth Horse Trials in 1970. PHOTO: CYRIL DIAMOND

thought it was the biggest course I had ever seen. I was worried about the spreads, which were not Doublet's strong point, but on the day I had a very good ride round the steeplechase, which was really heartening for my morale because we got round in time which I hadn't managed to do before. Also this didn't put too much strain on Doublet which was encouraging, especially as he proved he was very fit by recovering extremely quickly afterwards.

"Then, when I'd jumped the first cross-country fence, it was patently obvious that he was out to enjoy himself. I don't recall ever having such a smooth and remarkable ride, other than at Luhmühlen in 1975 with Goodwill. It was strange that

85

I didn't feel I was going very fast, yet obviously I didn't lose much time. Every time I approached a fence and said 'pay attention,' and asked him to check or go on, he responded. One of his great strengths was his accuracy in terms of jumping corners and angled fences. I didn't have to worry, just to line the fences up for him and we were safely over. The one moment of concern came at the Trout Hatchery."

At this famous obstacle where so many world-class riders have encountered problems, Doublet had some difficulty retaining both impetus and equilibrium in the water, but the Princess slipped the reins, sat quietly back in the saddle giving Doublet every chance to regain his balance and the one doubtful moment of a round, hallmarked by great courage and precision, was behind her. Doublet returned the second fastest time of the day – a remarkable feat. Only Stewart Stevens and Classic Chips, who invariably went like the wind across country, were faster.

Doublet's polished dressage test had given him the lead, which he now retained without difficulty across country. The Princess, however, was still not at all convinced that this comfortable lead would be a help, and the twenty-four hours before the final show-jumping round were very worrying, especially because she knew she should be able to go clear. "I tend to worry before every phase, but not so much the dressage. If you are over worried, you can make your horse overreact or very tense and it doesn't help you because things are apt to happen in the dressage arena about which there is very little you can do. In cross-country one is always jazzed up. I find show-jumping very trying because it's immediately obvious to everyone watching what is going on, you have already done quite a lot of hard work and a tiny mistake can be so magnified. Doublet wasn't the world's greatest show-jumper but again he rose to the occasion because he was that type of showman and sensed the occasion."

Doublet's sparkling clear round made the Princess the new European Champion. It was a splendid achievement to win from a field which included several leading Olympic riders in her first international competition when only just twenty-one years old.

1972, the year of the Munich Olympics, was not a good one for Doublet as tendon trouble kept him out of action at a critical time when he would certainly have been considered for a place in the British team.

At Badminton, in 1974, Doublet produced his now customary first-class dressage test but then fell on the steeplechase course. Only a few weeks later when Princess Anne was schooling him in Windsor Great Park, he fractured a bone in his hind leg and had to be put down.

Princess Anne's top horse was now Goodwill, who had finished fifth at Badminton that year. He was a completely different horse and coming to terms with him gave the Princess even more satisfaction than winning the European title because she now had so much more experience and knew what she was aiming to do.

Goodwill was seven years old when the Princess first had him and already had a history of his own having been the champion working hunter at the Horse of the Year Show and also been show-jumped by Alison Dawes. He is by Evening Trial out of the non-thoroughbred mare Mrs. Connor.

"On occasion, I despaired of ever getting him to do anything in the dressage arena and his show-jumping proved fairly sketchy and erratic. But his cross-country was never any trouble. It was very curious, my only problem was that he was so much on his forehand. I used to get very tired. It wasn't a question of stopping him, but of approaching a fence with a certain amount of control and balance so that he could get off the ground.

"Eventually, Goodwill's center of gravity was moved back a little, largely by using a gag bit. This has altered his whole way of crossing the country and he gallops better and is much more economical than before." The Princess now seldom uses the gag.

One of the main dressage hazards was the new experimental test that was used and included a flying change. "This came

H.M. the Queen's talented Columbus ridden by Princess Anne
makes nothing of the Tidworth steeplechase course in May, 1972.
PHOTO: CYRIL DIAMOND

much too soon for him, because he thought flying changes meant show-jumping, and I lost him completely and hardly dared to attempt the movement. Without a doubt, he was upset by arenas and large collections of people. They definitely worried him although with a horse it's difficult to tell if it's excitement or fear. He is now less affected by these conditions in that he will listen to you, but just as much in that you can feel him changing completely, as at Montreal in the Games, when this happened long before he actually arrived in the arena. Part of the problem there was that the horses had no idea what they were going into. There was a high bank between the collecting ring and the arena and, although we'd been allowed to work at the back, because of that big dividing bank they had not previously even caught a glimpse of where they were going, all the people or heard the noise, because they were shut away from them. Goodwill knew there was a dressage test to come, he had been very good outside, but when he entered the arena, he was taken by surprise and completely froze."

Since her marriage, when the horses have been stabled adjacent to her home – at first Sandhurst and now Gatcombe Park in Gloucestershire – the Princess has been quite happy to lend a hand when they are short staffed and this has also given her the opportunity to get to know her horses really well. "In the stable, I find Goodwill is much more friendly than he was, but he's still not what I'd call a chatty horse, he doesn't always come to see you. But, he's very nice in the stable and easy to do."

Goodwill may have given Princess Anne "rather tired fingers" the first time he carried her round Badminton in 1973, but he also gave her a very good ride to finish fifth. The Princess rode him carefully because, as he is quite a heavily built horse, she was not certain that he would have the necessary speed and stamina. But at the end of cross-country day, she was impressed by how little he had taken out of himself.

At Kiev in the Ukraine in 1973, Princess Anne was chosen to defend her European title as an individual riding Goodwill. "He was inexperienced in that he'd only done one three day event beforehand, but we had already come to the conclusion that size-wise, the obstacles should not be any problem to him because he had so much scope. I had a marvelous ride round the steeplechase which I wasn't expecting; he did it easily in the time. It was one of those days, at the start of the cross-country, when I didn't feel anything very much, which is usually a bad sign for me and means that something is going to go wrong. As it happened, I had my plans changed, and with the advantage of hindsight it was my inexperience, not his, that counted against us that day. If in the future it is suggested to me that I should jump a fence a different way from how I walked it, I would not do so. After all the falls at Fence 2 (a wide spread over a deep ditch), I was told that the bank on the take-off side had given way a bit, that it was now slightly dangerous and that this had made the spread much bigger. I went round along the side of the hill and turned at right angles to it and quite simply got it wrong. If I'd been three yards further up, or three yards further down, it would have been all right."

Even though Goodwill slowly and agonizingly tipped over onto his right side on landing, the pair very nearly made it. "The curious thing about it was that I think that Goodwill thought he'd made it. Sometimes you can tell with a horse, by the way he takes off, then they suddenly 'go' and you feel their legs start to stretch, but he never did that. When he reached the back pole, his legs were actually underneath him, which was very unusual, so his toes caught on the back pole because they had nowhere to go and this pitched him straight onto his nose. He was well above the jump and if he'd been three yards higher up the hill, he'd have had a little more speed and been that much nearer the fence because I got in $2\frac{1}{2}$ strides instead of 2 or 3. I now think if I'd been more experienced, I'd not have changed my riding plans, but that's something that unfortunately one learns the hard way. I still think it strange that the fence caused as much trouble as it did. The day we all walked the course, no one had been especially worried about it.

"I decided that as Goodwill had hit the ground very hard, and I couldn't stand on one leg because it had gone numb and disappeared from my hip to my knee, that I certainly wasn't going to achieve anything by carrying on as I was not a member of the team. It was not a sensible policy to continue at that stage of Goodwill's career. It was not until I'd been standing about for ten minutes that my shoulder suddenly began to hurt, and apparently that was my shoulder bone sinking back into its socket. It was a disappointing day because I thought it was basically a well-built course with some interesting fences, and trouble, other than at the now notorious Fence 2 proved well distributed."

1974 was a world championship year. Goodwill finished fourth at Badminton and the Princess was duly selected to ride as an individual for Great Britain in the championships at Burghley. On the steeplechase course, the Princess thought that Goodwill had broken down. He jumped the Open Ditch the second time around and almost pulled up in the next stride. She let him trot and he sorted himself out but despite this incident finished this section with only four time faults. "But when we set off on the cross-country, he wasn't quite himself; he was all right but wouldn't lengthen going into fences, which is most unusual for him. Afterwards, Mr. Scott-Dunn [the British team veterinary surgeon] said he'd been very lucky because he'd struck into himself, right on the back of the tendon sheath rather than to one side which I think might have caused a lot of trouble. He was very sore on it after that. We got round but he didn't feel right although he wasn't lame. When we had difficulty at the Double Coffin because he got a back foot in the second ditch which left him no room, I knew something must be wrong because for him combinations are usually no problem. At the drops such as the Dairy Mound and Waterloo Rails, he went straight down, just like a stone, which is again most unusual because he normally jumps well out over drops. Coming back over the Trout Hatchery, I thought he was going to stop. Instead of approaching from a canter as he usually does, he fell into a trot and jumped it from nothing, hurdling the entry log. Looking back, I can only give him full marks for getting round with this injury. To me it was a very impressive round; until then he'd never been facing so much trouble so one didn't know how he'd react to a tougher situation. He certainly showed he was very brave, was keen to look after himself and was not going to do anything stupid."

Despite this mishap, Goodwill finished twelfth. The United States wrested the team title from Great Britain and U.S.

Princess Anne on H.M. the Queen's Goodwill making her first appearance as a member of the British team and negotiating the

rider Bruce Davidson became world champion with Irish Cap.

The following year, 1975, Badminton was washed out, which hardly mattered to the Princess because Goodwill's jumping ability across country was beyond doubt. The European Championships were to be held at Luhmühlen, near Luneberg south of Hamburg in Germany, the following August. Princess Anne was selected to be a member of the British team. It was a remarkable team because for the first time ever all the British team members were women – Lucinda Prior-Palmer, Janet Hodgson and Sue Hatherly.

Although beforehand she thought she'd be so far behind after the dressage test that what happened afterward wouldn't matter, the Princess, nevertheless, looked forward to going to Germany for the competition. She was now more experienced and would be well able to have a go once Goodwill had his

water complex at Luhmühlen, West Germany in 1975.
PHOTO: FRANCIS SWIFT

dressage test behind him. However, there was not nearly such an arena atmosphere for the dressage as she had expected in Germany and the spectators were surprisingly calm and controlled for such an important event. The fact that they were only allowed on one side of the arena also proved helpful and beneficial to Goodwill who produced a far better test than she had dared hope.

In Luhmühlen the teams began competing rather earlier than is the usual custom. The Princess, who was laboring under a very heavy cold, found herself setting off on the steeplechase course at 9.30 a.m. The track was unusually twisty, but this served to steady up Goodwill, make him wonder where he was going next and he went very well. Just as she finished, news of Janet Hodgson's second fall from Larkspur came through on the loudspeaker and this made

93

the Princess suddenly aware that it would not be long before she started and that her round across country would now be of vital importance to the British team.

Goodwill then proceeded to give her a superb ride across country. Course designer Wolfgang Feld had produced a very complex water jump with two alternatives, the one favored by the British team lying to the right and ending with an up-turned boat. A sizeable part of the huge crowd had decided that this would prove the place to see some action. They were straining against the ropes and packed precariously on open farm carts as Goodwill, going strongly and very much on-ward bound came into view. Princess Anne described her passage:

"The water provided the moment that as usual probably looked horrifying. I must admit that I consider it was entirely my fault. As we drew close I thought he's going to stand-off going in and there will be a very big splash. But I had underestimated Goodwill. He showed much more sense than I did at that moment and had no intention of doing any such thing; he slipped in an extra stride, jumped it perfectly well and I was left hanging out of the back."

This fence came early on and during the rest of the round there was not a single moment of doubt. The course suited Goodwill particularly well because there were places where his endless scope could be used to great advantage to make up time. The awkward little corner with a Normandy Bank out was the type of obstacle that catches his interest and of which he makes light on account of his tremendous power and ability.

"It is not often I have the chance to enjoy a ride as it happens but on this occasion I did. I suppose it was a sign that things were going well, I had time to plan and didn't have to make any panic decisions. I was most impressed by the speed with which Goodwill got round because it was a relatively long course, quite fast, and Goodwill is not clean bred by any bounds of the imagination. He ended full of running, pulling like a train."

It is quite clear that the partnership was by then so cemented and Goodwill so clever across country that it must give a great feeling of confidence to set off on him in this phase, in which it would not be elaborating to describe him as one of the world's best.

His partner says: "After such a ride I feel reluctant ever to consider crossing such a course on another horse. Certainly my future horses will have a tremendous amount to live up to. Doublet wasn't so difficult because although he was not so scopey, he transmitted a feeling of confidence because you could be sure he would make a whole-hearted attempt at any fence. But on the other hand, you did not feel that he could jump anything from anywhere which I unquestionably get with Goodwill. He is so extraordinarily athletic that it doesn't seem to matter how we arrive at a jump, so long as he is pointed in the right direction he manages to arrive safely on the other side. Funnily it doesn't feel as awkward as one might expect. Certainly over a big course he is thinking so much himself that he doesn't leave you in a position where you are hanging onto the buckle hoping for the best, which I find very good for the morale."

The show-jumping course, built by Munich architect Mickey Brinckmann was ideal for Goodwill, being interesting, solid and quite big. Brinckmann's courses are always lavishly decorated with flowers and the banks of African marigolds and an unusual obstacle surmounted by a stork's nest made it look sufficiently different to catch and hold Goodwill's attention.

His clear round clinched the individual silver medal for the Princess in addition to a silver team medal with Lucinda Prior-Palmer and Sue Hatherly, as Janet Hodgson was severely shaken and had been forced to retire. If Sue and Harley had not unexpectedly fallen in the show-jumping, the latter medal could conceivably have been gold.

In 1976, the pair were excused from competing at Badminton but instead asked by the Selection Committee to prove themselves sufficiently fit for the Olympic Games. This they duly accomplished and were selected to be members of the British team.

At Bromont in Canada, fate did not smile on the Princess during the vital cross-country section. The very twisty course, ground changes, sharp corners and bumps and hills were not well suited to Goodwill and seemed likely to provide him with some very hard work. But, despite this, up to Fence 19, a zig-zag over a ditch where he fell, Goodwill had gone surprisingly quickly and obediently. "It wasn't that hideous a fence; you could kick on and the last thing I remember was seeing my stride and that it was wrong. So he was then left with one and a half strides instead of two and was going too fast to be able to do anything about it. After the inevitable sinking feeling I have no further recollection of what happened. I knew it would be disaster."

Horse and rider fell heavily on the landing side of the fence. After recovering from the shock, when they gathered themselves together, Princess Anne remounted and with the now traditional courage of the English female riders, she completed the course on Goodwill who had lost a front shoe during this incident. She does not remember any more details of the fall or finishing the course. Months later she was interested to observe in the film of the event that she tackled the step jump toward the end of the course a different way from how she planned when walking the course. Her first memory is of having her boots pulled off in the stables a quarter of an hour after passing the finishing post.

A clear round show-jumping finally placed Goodwill twenty-fourth. The British team failed to finish as Richard Meade, who finished fourth on Jacob Jones, was the only other British rider to complete the Olympic Three Day Event, since both Lucinda Prior-Palmer's Be Fair and Hugh Thomas's Playamar broke down.

It was a disappointing end to years of hard work and planning, especially as few horses last for two Olympic Games in this most gruelling sport and by the Moscow Games in 1980 Goodwill will be fifteen years old. His competitive life was

H.M. the Queen presenting the Raleigh Challenge Trophy to Princess Anne after she won the individual European Championship on Doublet at Burghley in 1971. A delighted Prince Philip watches.
PHOTO: CYRIL DIAMOND

probably lengthened as he was rested throughout the 1977 fall season prior to the birth of the Princess's son.

At the start of 1978, the Princess's other event horses were the brilliant Flame Gun, whose career has been checkered as he is very accident-prone, and two novices, Inchiquin, who is Irish, and Golden Reel. There will of course be others. When Princess Anne looks for a new horse, she does not have an entirely fixed pattern, but in essence looks for a horse with

97

the quality, speed and staying power to be good enough to win the Cheltenham Gold Cup. It must have brains and the movement necessary for dressage. Above all, the Princess's horses "Must be brave, have jumping ability and want to go across country almost from the beginning of their training. Three day events take enough out of a horse without it always working to its limit, so it is an advantage to have something to spare and not have to work flat out all the time." Princess Anne is not too concerned about shape, size or color, providing the horses are bold and possess the correct physical conformation which should help them to stay sound.

When she is actually competing, the Princess does not think she conspicuously enjoys any phase. "It rather depends on the horse and the day. Doublet's dressage was so consistent that I could enjoy riding my test on him, but there are very few horses that are entirely consistent in any one phase, so one frequently experiences some degree of worry."

Regarding the participation of women in the sport, the Princess considers there are both advantages and disadvantages concerning weight and the type of horses they can ride in terms of sheer strength. "Competing at international level and possessing the ability to treat such an event as just another competition must be largely a matter of experience, rather than getting very nervous and wound up beforehand, perhaps because this is one's first ride at international level.

"Physical courage is partially a question of strength so there is no argument, men are just stronger. The only question is whether girls should be thrown back into the saddle after a heavy fall. Obviously that's a matter of opinion and the only one I consider difficult. If there is a ground crew of men, they might well put up a man but have second thoughts about a girl.

"Weight is one of our advantages because many of the men who ride in three day events find it difficult to do 11 stone 11 pounds. Another advantage is that women tend to have very strong partnerships with horses, usually more so than men. This means that when they start to go well, the chances are they will continue to do so for quite a long time because they are really in tune together. This may be partly because they get more chance to ride than the men so the partnership develops further."

This last factor does not really apply to Princess Anne to the same extent as other women riders because of her official duties. Although as a child she had her own pony, she has had the advantage of riding all sorts of different ponies and horses from her earliest days in the saddle and this continued when she was at school. Now, she doesn't really mind what she rides, providing it doesn't pull.

The Princess likes to group her major official duties away from the competitive months but obviously this is not always possible and she does take on certain commitments during the spring and fall seasons. On such occasions, she tries to maintain her fitness by riding at least one horse and probably giving it some dressage schooling quite early in the morning before she sets out for the day's assignment.

When Princess Anne has a whole day to herself, she usually starts riding at 8.30 a.m. She may well exercise three horses but does not think it is possible to school thoroughly more than two horses on her own in a morning. She likes the chance to help in the stables in the afternoon, finding the opportunity to get to know the horses in another environment very useful, especially as some horses are so different in their boxes.

With the experience that Princess Anne and her husband, Captain Mark Phillips, now have behind them, there is no doubt they will continue to turn out a string of winners from their home.

Katherine Voss

Racehorse Trainer

As DAWN BREAKS and an early morning fog rolls over the track and creeps around the barns, a slim, dark-haired woman prepares for the daily routine of galloping the horses in her care. There are many women trainers in the United States, often eight or nine attached to each race track, but this is Katie Voss from Monkton, Maryland who, although only in her late twenties, has already proved herself to be one of the best. Her greatest success to date came with her father, John Merryman's, Twixt, who is to date the ninth record money winning filly of all time with $619,000 to her credit. When she was retired to stud at the end of 1975, Twixt had won a total of eighteen stakes.

Katie had the archetypal equestrian background and virtually grew up on horses. She was a member of the local Pony Club and hunted. By the time she was at Goucher College, Maryland, she had begun to feel very interested in training racehorses. At home on the farm, there were always a few flat horses about as her father was very keen on breeding and each year there was always a promising crop of youngsters.

Eventually, Katie found herself with a string of eight horses to train and she was fortunate enough to be able to hire the help of an expert, Nat Johnson, who was first to be her teacher and is now her good friend and training colleague.

Nat had worked all around Maryland, had considerable valuable experience and held an old trainer's license. Now, the pair always pool their opinions, so covering each other and between them, they miss very little.

Katie trains and stables the horses in her charge at Pimlico, some twenty-five minutes from her home. Personal attention and care throughout each and every day is very much a part of her philosophy and one of the reasons why she continues to turn out winners.

Each day begins with riding out horses. Many American trainers start work in the dark, but Katie firmly believes in waiting until the first light of dawn, so the horses do not rely entirely on instinct for direction, but can see where they are going and the exact footing for their daily work-out.

She usually rides out seven horses a day, working the horses in pairs and riding alongside another woman. The Orebanks racing establishment employs a total of six men and four women. The gallops usually start at 6.30 each morning and must end by 10 a.m. when the track closes. The horses are always walked home slowly, not only to relax and cool them, but to give a chance to consider their immediate form and the work necessary.

On a typical morning, the horses are then done up and fed. Katie inspects every horse on a thorough tour with Nat. If necessary, the veterinary surgeon is called and arrangements are made for the farrier. Very great attention is paid to the horses' legs and hoofs because in the sport of kings the old adage "no foot no horse" is the one to observe above all other.

The race tracks where she runs horses most regularly are Pimlico, Laurel, Bowie, Delaware Park in the summer, and Timonium in January and February, when Laurel is closed, and again in June and July.

Katie usually takes the horses to the race track herself, driving the Orebanks box and taking a helper in case of emergency but doing much of the pre-race preparation herself.

In late October 1977, Katie was due to run a mare called Catabias at Laurel. It was an afternoon of incessant rain as I drove down Whiskey Bottom Road to the stable gate entrance to meet her in the barn area. The huge gray glass-fronted stand stood prominent in the distance, the roof shrouded in mist like an ocean liner in harbor.

John D. Schapiro, President of Laurel Race Course, which is set in the scrub pine of Anne Arundel County, barely a stone's throw from the busy Washington D.C. Beltway, has built the track into one of the United States' most prestigious, cosmopolitan, and illustrious since he envisaged a global Grand Prix in 1951. The horses that compete in the Laurel International are only able to enter by invitation and represent the top of the three-year-old crop in the Far East, Europe, Australia and the Americas, indeed, anywhere a horse hits the headlines, and its achievements indicate it is right out of the ordinary.

As Katie led Catabias down the ramp, it was obvious that she had worried during the hour-long journey to Laurel. The mare stood in her stable, coat damp with sweat, looking anxiously about until a glycerine and peppermint mixture was sprayed into her mouth to help relax her. She was then led round the barns by her trainer until she had cooled down.

Everyone she passes seems to know Katie and to have a cheerful word for her. It is easy to understand why she says she has never experienced any antipathy since she began to train horses in what remains predominantly a man's world.

After continuous rain, the sand-based course becomes really deep and the horses make sizeable tracks as they gallop past in the race prior to that of Catabias while we wait for a lift across to the paddock from the patrol car.

All around there are horses coated in sandy loam up to their chests and bellies, looking as though they have been through some new therapeutic sand bath, and about to be hosed down and dried off.

The round-roofed covered paddock is alive with owners and their guests waiting for their horses to arrive and be saddled up. Unlike most English paddocks, other racegoers cannot see the horses inside. There are open stalls around the inner wall for taking off the rugs, but Catabias, who never likes the sensation of being enclosed in strange surroundings, at first refuses to enter. Jockey Bill Passmore arrives and receives last minute instructions from Katie. Catabias, who has already won

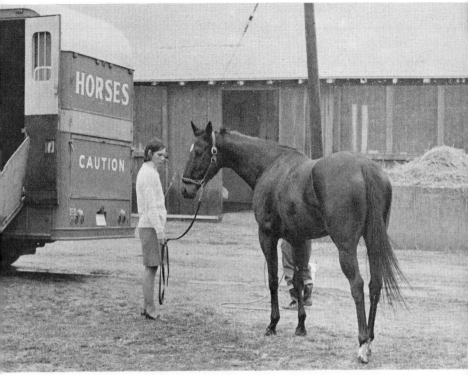

Trainer Katie Voss has just unloaded Catabias prior to racing at Laurel Race Track, Washington, D.C. PHOTO: FRANCIS SWIFT

a race this season, clearly needs an outing, but must be in with a chance although she is still fretting with tell-tale dark wet patches breaking out on her neck.

The conversations and last minute orders are punctured as the paddock judge's voice rises lazily, "Riders up."

Wished well by Mrs. Merryman, deputizing for her owner husband, Passmore, wearing the family colors, white, red hoops, red sleeves and quartered cap, is legged up. Soon Catabias is parading, mane and tail tossing against the back-cloth of flags and the central infield lakes where the resident ducks are alone in enjoying the continual downpour.

The lead horses appear, fleshy and strong, little bigger than ponies, an Appaloosa among them, ready to carry out the peculiarly North American custom of restraining the horses about to race and to prevent the jockeys from wasting their energy tugging on the reins or being decanted by a fractious horse on the way to the start.

Each racehorse paired with a lead horse, they alternately walk and canter their way to the gate half a mile away on the far side of the track. Now partially obscured by sheeting rain, the horses seem gradually to diminish in size, and habitual racegoers feel for their binoculars.

The starter watches the field approaching. Years of experience have taught him to assess a horse's likely reaction more quickly than even its trainer. He has the tools for the job and knows exactly when to use them, such as long bowed tongs to fit around the nose of any errant horse likely to resist by sitting down, rearing or striking out.

Loading into the starting gate that afternoon presents little trouble. Some jockeys are never ready and there are frantic shouts of "Not yet, not yet." Soon the great white gate moves, releasing a flood of horses which lunge past the protective aluminum pontoons as they drop their heads, bend their legs and are on their way.

All trainers experience the good and the bad days. For Katie the race is to prove perplexing. After showing on the bend prior to the final straight, Catabias fades to finish out of the first three.

Katie's immediate concern is with what went wrong. Why did the mare fail to produce her best form? Hurrying to the weighing-in enclosure, she has a quick word with her jockey, and then, as Nat Johnson arrives to take over, goes to the official administration block where, minutes after the race ends, a video-recording is played on the television screen, giving trainers a chance to analyze a close-up of how their horses ran.

There are several possible reasons for the problem. Was the mare slightly amiss? Has she contracted some virus, or at five years old is she losing her enthusiasm for racing? Did she need an outing a shade more than seemed apparent? Although she usually performs well on heavy going, was it even more de-

The very heavy going at Laurel Park which proved too much for Catabias trained by Katie Voss. PHOTO: FRANCIS SWIFT

manding than it appeared? Katie considers all these points.

One filly in the race has broken down beyond recall and will never see another race track; even saving her for stud is by no means a certainty. The most important fact for her trainer is that Catabias is sound and for her there will be another day.

But there is no more time for Katie to consider Catabias. Much business takes place at the tracks. A slim young jockey who regularly rides for her comes up and tells here where he will be available the following week. One of her horses should be just about ready to have a go and has two engagements; they discuss the likely opposition and where he is most likely to win. Life goes on.

Lorne McKean

Equestrian Sculptor

LORNE MCKEAN is the leading young British representational artist specializing in animal and portrait sculpture to emerge in the 1970s. She has a special talent for capturing the essential quality of her subject, combined with an inherent sense of composition.

She was born in Surrey, England, and moved to the United States as a child during World War II. After the war she returned to Great Britain and attended a private school until she was twelve years old. "I was lucky," she said, "because the headmistress taught Pythagoras and Plato, which meant that I learned that whatever field I eventually chose, a wide dimension of interpretation was possible."

Although she never discussed it openly, she never thought of doing anything other than art. From the age of seven onward her greatest pleasure was modeling in any medium that was available; more often than not it was soap or salt. "I didn't realize that I was actually sculpting, but I can remember very clearly at the age of ten being given a bag of clay. It was the most exciting present I have ever been given."

Lorne moved on to another school, then during her fourteenth year she suffered an attack of polio in her arm, back and neck. She was fortunate to recover entirely, but the complete cure took a year. First she spent six months in hospital, then six months at home where she continued her education with a governess. She had a pony at the time, and rode as part of her rehabilitation.

With her recuperation complete, her parents decided that

The John Pinches International Dressage Trophy designed and cast in silver, by Lorne McKean.

to attend a dancing school would be a good idea because the movement would continue to have a remedial and strengthening effect on their daughter. For Lorne the polio was "a blessing in disguise." She had been very unhappy at her previous school and found that she fitted in well and enjoyed life at her new school, Elmhurst Ballet School at Camberley in Surrey. On Saturdays she attended a local art school.

She left when she was sixteen years old, and filled in four months with a Cordon Bleu cookery course. She was so excited at the prospect of going to study in Florence that she remembers little of the culinary skills she was taught, recalling the course as a disaster. When she was seventeen years old she traveled to Italy.

In Florence, Lorne continued a general education, studying Italian, history of art, playing the piano and spending as much time as possible at a remarkable, tiny, drawing school. This was, and still is, run by Signorina Simi. Drawing is taught on exactly the same lines as in the days of the Medicis and the Renaissance era, and only Italian is spoken.

She spent scant time studying the many Florentine art treasures, preferring to devote as much time as possible to learning at the drawing school. "I learned all the drawing I know there."

Lorne's parents now realized that their daughter was channeled irrevocably toward art, and somehow managed to find the money for her to remain a total of six months longer in Florence. She recalls: "It wasn't that I knew that art was what I wanted to do, it was that I never thought of doing anything else. It was always sculpture and I loved animals."

On her return to England she spent four years at Guildford Art School; like so many artists Lorne is very individualistic and remembers this as a time of confusion.

"You began with a basic intermediate course, and at the end of that time took an exam. It would be equivalent to today's foundation course, but for me it was a complete waste because I was only interested in sculpture, and the type of drawing such as abstract ideas and imaginative forms were just dreams and fantasies so far as I was concerned. I felt that making photo-graphic copies and studying the history of art was standing still, but when I was able to go out with live models I felt that something of the life, fun and joy I experience when creating when I am sculpting was coming over me. What Guildford gave me was time, and I was fortunate to have a grant to go.

"There was one teacher there who was fantastic, and very helpful and useful to me at that stage of my career. He showed me that it was no good rushing out after ideas unless you could put them down. For example he would look at the corner of an eye and then say, 'Well, tell me, how does it work?' His name is Michael Rizzello and he is now President of the Royal Society of British Sculptors, although at the time he was just beginning teaching."

Lorne was then accepted into the Royal Academy Schools in London. She counts herself very lucky to have been accepted because having the final art school examination, the National Diploma of Design, is a normal condition of entry, and she had not even passed her Intermediate. However the same year she had had two pieces of sculpture accepted for the exhibition "upstairs" at the Royal Academy Summer Exhibition at Burlington House. One was a life-sized reclining figure and one a portrait head of a model whom she had seen dancing in a theater.

"At the end of my interview for the Royal Academy Schools I was asked as a formality, 'You have passed your final examin-ation, haven't you?' I replied with trepidation, 'Well, actually no, and I haven't passed my Intermediate either.' I needn't have worried because my interviewer thought this was hilariously funny and the qualification was waived."

She spent four years there, and during this time met the sculptor Edwin Russell who was eventually to become her husband. His past commissions include St. Catherine in Westminster Abbey, St. Michael in the Chapel of St. Michael, St. George in St. Paul's Cathedral and new figures twelve feet high to replace certain existing figures on the exterior of St. Paul's Cathedral.

"After I had been there some time we found a fabulous place called Haunch of Venison Yard. It was one little room that made an extraordinary studio, right at the top of many flights of stairs in a frightfully smart location right opposite Claridges Hotel. During my last four years' training I tried to do as much outside work as I could, which meant that in all my holidays and spare time I worked for the actual price of the casting. Then by the time I actually left the Academy I had several pieces round about in private houses. When people first come to any form of art they always want to know what work you've done to give them confidence. So when I was able to tell them where they could see pieces I was gradually able to start charging a little, and then a little more, until it became more realistic. This was encouraging because it meant that when my grant was dropped I would be able to make the transition over to sculpture without having to go and work somewhere like a coffee bar to make it possible. At about this time I did a bust of Sir Michael Redgrave, who found it very amusing to plough up all these stairs and sit in our little garret which we often garlanded with flowers. There was a very chic florist in the Yard and they used to give us their discards, often from the dustbins, so the studio frequently looked like a flower show."

A bust of Mr. Arthur Simon was one of her very first commissions. He was a friend of her parents and sat patiently for hours and hours. "In fact his bronze took me at least fourteen sittings, and completing it gave me a very great thrill."

By the time she left the Academy her special talent for composition, had been recognized, because she won the Leverhulme Scholarship, the Silver Medal for Sculpture combined with Architecture, and the Feodora Gleichen Scholarship.

"I had always loved sculpting animals, especially horses, but gradually I began to become increasingly interested in people. It meant that instead of recognizing the people by the animals, I started recognizing the animals by the people. This opened up the field because although all the possibilities are there in the animals there are also limits, and it represents an expansion when you move into people. With people, especially if you look into their eyes, you see the possibilities are there to be realized then, but with an animal they exist but are almost imprisoned in some place. I have done more horses than any other animals such as cheetahs, goats, cats and dogs, probably because so many people are interested in horses. I find that when I've done a racehorse and someone asks me to do a Welsh cob, although it is still a horse it is literally as good as sculpting a different animal. The variety in horses is enormous, even the range of character in just one breed."

When I talked with Lorne McKean she was demonstrating at the May Art in Action 1978 Exhibition at Waterperry House near Oxford. Her models, a large pair of Anglo-Nubian goats, one brown and one white with large droopy ears, were in a pen outside the marquee she shared with her husband, the animals being tended by their daughters, Rebecca aged twelve and Tanya who is ten. It was a sweltering Sunday. The day's exhibition should have closed an hour earlier, but the loud-speaker system had succumbed to the heat and the huge friendly crowd showed no inclination to go home. Earnest students, Leyland motor workers from nearby Cowley, school-children, housewives and the county gentry rubbed shoulders.

Earlier Lorne had modeled the goats in plasticine in front of a riveted crowd and the inevitable television cameras. The model was placed in the cool of the marquee. The medium chosen was plasticine because of the goats' fine legs and the problem of working in the heat. She prefers to work on the spot and carry the model around. Although plasticine is not so satisfying a medium to work in as clay, she elects to use it on such an occasion. To the amateur eye the impression is a blend of infinite power and yet delicacy, which will hopefully not sag in the sticky heat.

When she receives a commission the process follows a standard pattern. Recently, when she was asked to sculpt a Welsh cob, the first thing she did was go to Wales. "I had no idea in my head about what I was going to do, and that is

Lorne McKean's artistry is demonstrated by the statue of H.R.H. Prince Philip on his polo pony Portano, H.M. the Queen's personal silver wedding gift to her husband.

absolutely vital. What I must bear in my mind is exactly what I have been asked to do. This will be related to the size, and whether the person wants a very particular facet of the animal in question portrayed or whether they want a more general aspect, and also any relevant factors. For example they may specify that they would like the animal to be trotting, or leave it entirely to me.

"They may say remember the show people who say, 'It's not allowed to do that,' or if it's a pet animal and twists in a way the show people would consider incorrect, it just doesn't matter and the field is your own.

"I then arrive and look at the animal in as many different

aspects as possible, hoping to find possibilities that did not immediately come to light. It may be that I will decide to ride my subject, and go out with someone else riding another horse, or do this and change over horses half way. They may also lead my subject around for me to study. If it's a stallion it's very useful if it's turned out in a field and some mares are put out in the field with it. When a horse is just dozing at pasture it is hard to capture its character. This way it comes to life and one sees the full distillation of their possibilities. Through a tiny incident the essence of the animal itself may be revealed, and the theme of my sculpture suddenly becomes apparent. When this happens it's fine. It may not be from a momentary incident, it may be from a composite picture."

It doesn't matter which way the idea evolves. As soon as it does Lorne must capture it, and get it down in some medium before it changes or dulls in her mind.

Accordingly, she has always had some drawing wax with her, and puts up the idea as quickly as possible. Usually it takes only ten minutes to capture the little sketch that will be her bible for the assignment on hand, and the only thing that really matters. "It is easy to work away from the original idea and not to be aware of it, so it is vital as a guide line, and if my main sculpture crashed to the ground it would not be the end of the world. If I lost my first wax sketch it would be."

Now that the main idea is formed she likes to create it as quickly as possible. The first move is to put up the armature, the wire to support it, and then get going again quickly. That can be done in one of the two studios, one small and one large which she shares with her husband at their home near Hindhead in Surrey. She finds this is usually better done at home in the studio because, "At this stage, if you see more it usually clouds the issue.

"I then continue in the studio, but if I find I am putting in lifeless work or becoming repetitive I return to the animal to reestablish communication with my subject. If all goes well I stay in the studio until the work is finished." The medium used on the armature depends on the subject. She prefers to use clay, especially for a big project, because for a modeling medium there is nothing to beat it unless she has been asked for a carving. If the model has fine legs and the work is outside, plasticine is the choice, but if it is winter it can be wax which is preferable to plasticine but hopeless in any degree of heat.

She usually works from the idea and checks it from the wax model to ensure that she is not off course. If she worked from the wax model it would, she considers, be a copy of a copy. If the subject is a long way away from home she may well complete the clay model on site. "I always fear a certain laziness may creep in if I return to the studio, and I may not return at the crucial moment when I need to."

Lorne has sculpted two Welsh cobs, both from the famous Llanarth stud which has done so much to preserve the breed. The first was for the stud and was a bronze of Llanarth Braint, "which means honor and dignity, just the qualities he possesses, in Welsh."

Miss Doris Lindner, who established the brilliantly successful series of horses for the Royal Worcester Porcelain Company and also sculpted the bronze of the immortal chaser Arkle that stands at Cheltenham Racecourse, suggested that Lorne should do some figures for them. Llanarth Flying Comet is the first of a series of ponies sculpted by her which was due to be launched in 1978. "The difference between the two horses, although they are both Welsh cobs, is incredible. Many consider Comet to be the better animal, but Braint has that indefinable element of quality."

At the stage when the bronze is finished it goes to the bronze foundry where the complicated process of transforming the clay model into the finished bronze is carried out. There are few foundries where this fine task can be carried out. Lorne uses either Art Bronze in Chelsea, who do the bulk of her work, or Galizia in Battersea.

The process favored by Lorne is the lost wax process. Because she works on commission for an edition, so she can have an exhibition and other editions to sell, a cold rubber mold is taken because it takes better detail than a hot rubber mold, and results in a rubber negative. Into this, liquid wax is poured, swilled around and poured out. Then the rubber is taken off, leaving a positive wax cast $\frac{1}{8}-\frac{1}{4}$ inch thick. At this stage the middle is empty, and into it is poured the core, composed of a material called ludo, which is a mixture of dead plaster and brick dust.

"This is the old-fashioned method which may be slow but is by far the best with a special quality of its own. At this stage I work the wax which is not very common at this time. As it has been through a mechanical process it is a little deadened and loses a little life, and has a slightly soapy quality. I work it until it comes alive again. There are various details such as the seams to deal with, although the foundry know me so well now that they usually do this for me. The foundry then put another mold on the wax. It is made of a material hard enough so that when it is put in the kiln it fires hard enough to take the bronze that is then poured into the space. When it is fired the wax melts out, which is why it is called the lost wax process."

What then remains is a core inside, a space where the wax was, and the mold outside. The liquid bronze, which has been poured into a crucible and heated, is then poured into that space. Now there is core inside, with bronze and mold outside. The final move when the metal has hardened is to chip and brush off the mold from the outside, and there is the bronze. The material inside is washed out and a hollow bronze remains.

Lorne then works this, a practice called chasing which used to be standard but is seldom done these days. "I do this not because the cast is not superb but because life is lost in the various processes."

The final stage is applying a patina. In twenty years the bronze would acquire its own patina from the chemicals in the air. If it were by the sea it would go greenish, and in other conditions it might go brownish, blackish or even reddish. Of course people won't wait twenty years so chemicals are used that are naturally in the air, such as sulphur and ammonia, and applied to the bronze, so obtaining the color appropriate to where the bronze will stand. All that then

Lorne McKean with a bust of the Earl of Lichfield, commissioned by the BBC. PHOTO: PAMELA BOOTH

remains is the mounting and waxing; a good patina takes about six months to settle.

While Lorne has studied anatomy she does not consciously use her technical knowledge, feeling that if she does she will only be on the surface. "Hopefully my figures are anatomically correct. I seldom use photographs, even to check. I do know if something looks wrong and if it doesn't flow."

By this time consuming process she has already produced over two hundred different bronzes, although she is never aware of rushing through a commission. She has had four exhibitions at the Sladmore Gallery in London, the first being held in 1969. This largely contained bronzes based on initial ideas of her own, but clearly she prefers working to a commission. "If someone says 'I'd like this,' it stops me going off into dreams of my own, and I find it actually freeing to work under those conditions and less limiting than working on what one always fears may be just a little idea one has had."

Since the first exhibition, Lorne has had no shortage of the commissions she needs for the continuation of her art.

After her first sculptures were accepted by the Royal Academy she has continued to exhibit there regularly. In 1972 she was elected a Fellow of the Royal Society of British Sculptors, and in 1969 to the Society of Portrait Sculptors.

Her work can be found in collections all over the world, especially in France, North and South America, Malaya and South Africa. Her most important commissions include "H.R.H. Prince Philip on his Polo Pony Portano," Her Majesty the Queen's personal silver wedding gift to her husband, the John Pinches International Dressage Trophy which is cast in silver, portraits of Professor Courant of the Institute of Mathematical Sciences in New York, Lord Salisbury at Hatfield House, and the Pegasus Sculpture at Miami, Florida.

Mrs. Pamela Carruthers

Course-Designer

IT IS MAY 1, 1978 and the first May Day bank holiday in Great Britain. The salt tinged rain which has lashed across Douglas Bunn's great international show-jumping arena at Hickstead in Sussex for over twenty-four hours shows no sign of abating. The bowler hatted Master of Hickstead and his course-designer, Mrs. Pamela Carruthers, who is almost unrecognizable in black sou'wester and olive-green oilskins, sit together on the observation platform in the center of the arena as a series of Grade C horses splosh by, coping remarkably well with the deep-holding and adverse going.

The well drilled Junior Leaders of the Royal Corps of Transport are grappling with the extremely difficult conditions most successfully, quickly replacing knocked-down poles.

Despite the mud the course is proving just right for these inexperienced horses, and the whole operation is running like clockwork as cars pull into the ground from the busy London–Brighton road hoping to get a good place to watch some of the world's leading riders contest the Embassy Grand Prix. They are scheduled to include the reigning European champion, Holland's Johan Heins, Graham Fletcher from Yorkshire and David Broome. Broome has just driven in after flying back from winning the Rome International Horse Show Championship on Tabac Original (the former Heatwave) and yet another car for the Leading Rider award.

Hours of concentrated planning have produced this effortless pattern. Five months ago, in January, Mrs. Carruthers worked out all the course plans for this meeting with her

Course-designer Pamela Carruthers walking the course at Hickstead with Prince Philip, President of the F.E.I. and Douglas Bunn, the Master of Hickstead. PHOTO: LESLIE LANE

second-in-command at Hickstead, Jon Doney. The order for necessary material was then put in to Hickstead. At this stage the distance of the combinations are established, but the heights are decided when the course is actually built because they are dependent on the going and the class of entry. A plan is also sent ahead to Hickstead so that the material can be prepared.

There are four stages. First Mrs. Carruthers puts out the jump numbers in their exact situation. Jon Doney follows and erects the frames of the fences. Regular assistant, Richard Jeffery, then brings out the material and puts the necessary pieces by each number. The fourth and final crew then fill in the jumps to the given specification.

Each evening before the show opens there is a television conference which Mrs. Carruthers attends to ensure that timing and positioning of jumps will fit in with the television producer Fred Viner's coverage plans.

As the prize winners come in to collect their awards, conditions continue to deteriorate. Douglas Bunn and Mrs. Carruthers confer as patches of water start to appear where the horses' hoofs have dented the smooth turf on the take-off side of the jumps. A telephone call to the weatherman at Shoreham from where the rain is coming confirms that heavy rain will continue for the entire afternoon. The outcome is obvious, and as the international riders enter the ring to walk the Grand Prix course the announcer's voice rings out from the loudspeakers, "The show has had to be abandoned."

Initially the riders are disappointed. "Just for a few spots of rain," several of them are heard to grumble, but the wisdom of the decision is self-evident an hour later as still more water lies on the arena surface and the sky is an even darker gray. By the time the huge palaces on wheels with their sponsors' names emblazoned on their sides rumble out of the mud, carrying the international show-jumpers north toward London and home a few hours early, the riders all concur: "Pam did the right thing."

As the only woman course-designer who works full time at an international level, Mrs. Carruthers has the distinction of being very much alone in a man's world. It is a challenge she relishes and which she faces with the spirit which has been characteristic of her since she was a teenager in the late 1930s.

When Pamela Torrie was fifteen years old and displaying the passion for horses experienced by countless schoolgirls of this age, her parents decided that the best way to break, or at least modify, their daughter's enthusiasm would be a spell at a French finishing school, and she duly crossed the English Channel to study at the Ozanne's in Paris.

They had not reckoned on their daughter's determination.

She soon achieved an introduction to some of the leading French riders at a time when France was enjoying great international success in the sport. A year later, when she was sixteen, she rode horses for two top team members, Laissradière and Bizard, at the Paris Horse Show. She also rode the French team horses in ladies classes in 1937 and 1938, though eventually such opportunities ceased because she returned to England.

During the time she was in Paris she wrote home to both her mother and grandmother, telling them how cold the weather was, and how badly she needed a fur coat. Without consulting each other they both instantly dispatched a check to this end. The money was used to purchase a two-year-old racehorse, Peace Pay, who then traveled back to England with her new owner.

Mr. and Mrs. Torrie had now, not surprisingly, given up hope of tearing their daughter away from horses. On her return to England she then turned to the world of the show horse, exhibiting hunters, hacks and cobs with considerable success. She won the hack class at Olympia, riding Peace Pay whom she had broken and produced herself.

Colonel Sir Harry Llewellyn had come to know Pamela quite well through his future wife, Teeny, a fellow pupil at the Ozanne's, and he now persuaded her to try her hand at show-jumping in England, finding her Galway Boy. She jumped this horse as a five- and six-year-old with the British team, but then decided to sell him as at that time women riders were not allowed to take part in Nations Cups (international team competitions) so the ultimate accolade was unachievable.

But then at the first Horse of the Year Show at Harringay, her outstanding Benjamin, who was established as the country's leading cob, was mysteriously poisoned. Deeply affected, she decided never to show again.

During the war, Pamela Torrie had married and become Pamela Carruthers. When her husband left her in 1952 she could not afford to continue competing in any equestrian field, and started course building at small local shows, hoping that this would at least enable her to continue hunting.

Using her international experience, she quickly progressed onward by means of trial and error, and soon proved her worth with invitations to build courses at the elegant Ascot Spring Show and then at the first Hickstead in 1960.

Douglas Bunn's invitation to design at Hickstead reflected his flair, imagination and intuition. His foresight and choice were to play a major role in establishing Hickstead as Britain's foremost permenent show-jumping arena, and simultaneously proved to be Pamela Carruthers' major breakthrough.

Strangely, Mrs. Carruthers was little recognized in Great Britain until in 1967 she accepted an invitation to build at Washington, D.C. This opened the North American Indoor Fall Circuit, where her courses met with immediate acclaim.

Jon Doney, who received his early training from her, and is now internationally known as a course-designer in his own right, has become her number one deputy. He was to build at the Washington International in 1978 while she worked in Iran, helping to establish international riders by designing at various shows leading up to the big International in Teheran. Jon Doney has also stood in at Hickstead on the rare occasions when Mrs. Carruthers has been absent, as for instance, when she broke her ankle, or one meeting in 1977 when she was at work in Australia and in 1978 when she was in Canada. Clashing dates are an increasing problem on the world circuit.

She has accepted course-designing invitations to Australia, Bulgaria, Canada, Denmark, France, Germany, Greece, Iran, Mexico, South Africa, South America and the United States. Now she derives particular pleasure from visiting less experienced show-jumping countries and from helping them to realize the requirements of a top show-jumping course. In February 1979 she is to visit Venezuela and Colombia and says, "If new countries want to develop show-jumping as a sport it is very important to do it the right way, and I really look forward to such opportunities. However I will always need the stimulus of working at major internationals such as Hickstead. If it were not for the advent of Hickstead I should not be where I am now."

1977 must rate as her most demanding year to date. Her calendar ran:

January:	At home, planning various courses.
February:	Tampa, Florida, International Classes.
April:	In California to discuss building new showground near Los Angeles. Fly on westward to Royal Show, Sydney, Australia. Melbourne for Two Day Clinic.
May:	Alberta, Western Canada, for Calgary Indoor, Edmonton, Red Deer and Spruce Meadows Meetings.
End June:	To England for Hickstead.
July:	Calgary for a week-long Junior Show at Spruce Meadows. Return home for Hickstead Nations Cup Meeting.
August:	Hickstead Derby Meeting.
Aug.–Sept.:	Rotterdam International Horse Show, Holland.
September:	Final Hickstead Meeting. Calgary International at Spruce Meadows, Calgary, featuring Grand Prix and Nations Cup. Two days' holiday visiting son who lives on Vancouver Island. Maple Ridge Show near Vancouver. Fly to Sacramento, California for one day to plan big new outdoor arena.
October:	Week at Cleveland, Ohio for Indoor Show. Judge Hunter Trials at Potomac Riding Center near Washington, D.C. Washington International Horse Show. Nations Cup. Grand Prix. Flew home by Concorde.
November:	On to Iran for a big international show at Tehran.
December:	Judged at the Paris International.

"As a woman working with men and doing what was previously regarded as a man's job, I must be more exact in the work I do because I can afford to make mistakes much less than men. However cross I may feel with occasional inefficient help, I have to remember never to let this show or slam any of my helpers.

"I get very worked up and tense during a class, because if I make a mistake I suffer continually right through the class, whereas for the riders and horses it's only a few minutes each. I am always very much on the rider's side.

"Originally I learned by putting into practice what I myself had been taught through jumping, and I think initially my courses were too jumpable. You never stop learning. Yesterday Graham Fletcher said to me, 'Your courses are not as big as they used to be,' and I think he's right. With lighter poles I can build more narrow fences and that is also better for the horses; heavy fences take too much out of them. In the mid-seventies, course building became too solid and heavy. The Montreal Olympics at Bromont were the ultimate of that type of course. It is very dangerous for the riders and horses if the course-builders don't know enough about the ability of the class of competitors for which they are designing."

She emphasizes that it is a real problem when a country has not as yet got the quality of horse in regular competition for course-builders to acquire the experience necessary to build courses for major championships or the Olympic Games. When she had just begun course-building she found the help she received from Jan Jurgens of Holland invaluable. In the early 1950s when she was beginning, she herself paid to go to the Rome International Horse Show to study top class courses and was very fortunate to be allowed into the ring.

She considers it vital that as the expansion of show-jumping continues all course-designers should have more chance to get together, such as at the meeting held in the spring of 1978 at Warendorf, the German National Equitation Center. Here she assisted the German Munich Olympic architect Mickey Brinckmann who took a seminar for representatives of twenty-seven countries, some inexperienced and some experienced. A regular pooling of ideas and demonstrations of trends is essential.

"When I first came to Hickstead I never dreamed it would help to give me such a wonderful life of travel. To traverse the world as I do, and have the opportunity of working with people of different countries, race, and creed, is far better to me than taking a holiday. I am fortunate enough to enjoy first-class travel and have friends all over the world, people with whom I stay whenever possible and who are also kind enough to house certain clothes until my next visit.

"It is strange that when I began to course-build, I did so in order to be able to hunt with my local pack, the Duke of Beaufort's, but now I am so busy that I find it hard to fit in any hunting. However, when I'm home I never fail to ride out every day. My mother, who is in her eighties, acts as my long-suffering secretary and keeps everything under control in my long absences."

It is obviously an exhausting occupation. Mrs. Carruthers may well be the world's most traveled course-designer and thus continual jet lag is an obvious problem, but that is only one reason why she frequently has to combat fatigue.

There is a high degree of strain and nervous tension caused by responsibility not only for all the courses but also for co-ordinating the preparation and maintenance of jumps throughout a meeting. The course must be ready for the walk round; the staff who erect the jumps must be well looked after and she has to be certain that they get their meals. Poles are heavy to lift and she is quick to pick them up herself when necessary. The jumps must be maintained at exactly the same dimensions throughout a competition.

It is quite reasonably a matter of some pride that the jump-off course at Hickstead is usually ready by the time the last competitor has left the ring. At Hickstead Douglas Bunn insists on the highest standards of presentation and Mrs. Carruthers totally agrees. This means that the jumps are freshly painted where necessary for each meeting, washed each morning *in situ* to move any dirt or mud that has splashed up, and the decoration material such as shrubs and flowers for in-filling and general overall effect is second to none in Great Britain. "Douglas always says, 'We are a spectator sport so the presentation of the jumps is all important.'"

Mrs. Carruthers' task of judging correctly the exact height, spread and distance at which she must set the fences in order to get the required number of clear rounds is a complex one. While there are certain principles to bear in mind, such as that a horse's stride is approximately twelve feet, and longer going downhill and shorter uphill, the exact result varies with different horses and different conditions such as thick mud.

"For the future, my aim is toward using slightly lighter poles and presenting more rider problems so that the horses will last a little longer. There can be no doubt that Hickstead has taught many people to become more aware. Many people can design very adequately for novices, but few possess the art and flair necessary to design courses at the top level."

Mrs. Carruthers considers the contact of talking to riders very necessary, saying, "The more I design courses, the more I am prepared to listen to the riders. I have learned who are the ones to listen to. I am also quick to apologize if I make a mistake. I never try to catch out horses; I always hope to achieve a good result."

Strangely, her desertion of the French finishing school now seems predestined. She reminisced, "I was sent to forget about horses and contrarily came home having learned to speak excellent French and a great deal about show-jumping. The language is of constant use to me now on different assignments, and in those early days I acquired a sense of fashion that helped me become aware how essential it is for women doing men's jobs to be immaculately turned out at all times."

In April 1978 Mrs. Carruthers most deservedly received a British Equestrian Federation Medal of Honour at a presentation at The Saddlers Hall, Cheapside, London.

Pamela Carruthers talking to U.S. rider Scott Nederlander at the Gold Cup Meeting in the J.F.K. Stadium, Philadelphia, September, 1978. PHOTO: FINDLAY DAVIDSON

Frances Rowe

Show-Jumping Trainer

IN THE POST-WAR ERA of show-jumping the sport has escalated from being a military activity, almost entirely participated in by officers of the world's leading cavalry schools (such as Weedon in Great Britain and Fort Riley in the United States), to a sport enjoyed by riders from a wide spectrum of society. Remarkably, there is only one woman trainer, Frances Rowe, whose riders are continually able to hold their own on an international level.

Frances' parents loved horses and one early memory is of her father, a keen amateur whip, and his trotting horses at the local county fair in Virginia. She began riding as a little girl, but whereas her father "just rode by the seat of his pants," she became increasingly involved in the correct approach and problems of riding when competing in junior division classes.

At the age of eighteen Frances went to college at Mary Washington, Fredericksburg, Virginia, where she majored in English. For three years, it was a case of Chaucer in the morning, helping as a basketball coach in the afternoon and somehow fitting in riding lessons from Russell Walther Senior, whose son now teaches in South Carolina.

After finishing college in 1947, she competed that summer as an amateur with two horses of her own, and also rode conformation hunters for Jack Payne, and for Mrs. Raymond Barbin.

She competed extensively as an amateur, combining riding with teaching English. In 1951 Frances turned professional. Her talent was soon recognized and thus clients came quickly and she was offered some good horses to ride. For a period she managed horses for Richard Reynolds of the aluminum company at Richmond, Virginia. At the time, he was Master of the Deep Run Hunt and rode to hounds three days a week. Frances, who also loved hunting, was able to widen her experience across country and still compete with Mrs. Barbin's show horses during the summer.

In the fifties the Virginia circuit was probably the toughest in the States; most of the top competition animals were centered in this area where the horse was still essential to the local way of life.

A quarter of a century later, the situation has gradually changed with Virginia still the home of foxhunting, but the top competition horses spread much more widely over the United States and the majority of the top Virginian show-hunters and jumpers in the care of Frances Rowe and show-jumping star Rodney Jenkins.

In 1955 disaster struck when Frances broke her neck in a bad fall which involved two vertebrae in the cervical region of her spine. At this time, the spinal fusion treatment later available was not in common use, so in an enforced change of direction, she abandoned show horses, simultaneously extending her range, training racehorses for five years on Richard Reynolds' farm, gradually breaking the yearlings and getting the two-year-olds ready to race. Her one regret at this time was that she was not able to enjoy the continuity of seeing them through to the racecourse.

During 1960 and 1961, she underwent two major back operations and during this period decided to set up her own establishment at Foxwood Farm, Crozier, Virginia.

Since that date, multi-millionaire Patrick Butler has been a continuous patron. Intensely interested in horses, summering in St. Paul, Minnesota and wintering in Florida, he really lives to see his horses jump, calling frequently to discuss their prospects and problems. "If we happen to be schooling at 5 o'clock in the morning, he just might be there."

Initially, Joannie Boyce, just out of junior classes and very promising, was Frances' only rider. She stayed at Foxwood eleven years before leaving to set up her own yard in Greensborough, North Carolina. The pair now work closely, traveling the shows together and often interchanging horses if best suited for the other stable's projects.

Two former Foxwood jockeys who now rate among America's top eight are Conrad Homfeld, who joined the stable after making his first trip to Europe with the United States Equestrian Team with Triple Crown, and Joe Fargis, a regular U.S.E.T. representative. Both were members of the United States team during the 1977 fall circuit and Joe was a member of the team which won the gold team medals at the 1975 Pan-American Games at Mexico City.

Frances' success as a trainer is attributable in considerable measure to the close psychological study she gives to her riders and horses. It is her prerogative as trainer to place a particular horse with a particular rider and to alter them when necessary and her judgment in this is a largely contributing factor toward the Foxwood horses remaining at the top. It is also interesting that her riders readily accept her decisions of change.

Balbuco was rated a fantastic athlete, a horse with the physical ability to jump high uprights, wide spreads or turn on a sixpence. He is, however, casual with his knees and slow in front and thus perfect for Conrad, who rode him with infinite patience. Frances' system of training is based on gaining the entire trust of the horse and Conrad, who has a very subtle seat, proved the ideal partner, clinging to his horse to the very last minute with perfect timing.

The ex-U.S.E.T. horse Old English knows everything that can be taught so with him all that is necessary is to keep him fit, feeling good and sweet-tempered. He has shelly, thin-walled front hoofs and at first proved hard to keep sound. A horse with great natural balance, he is never jumped with studs in front. In contrast to Balbuco, he is brave, with tidy knees and natural bounce.

Many of the horses in her stable arrived with temperament

problems, especially Caesar. He is a West Coast horse and, like many others from California, may have undergone a disorienting period of terror because out West the horses tend to be jumped too high too young, and often "hit with everything but the kitchen sink." Caesar was the mount of Joe Fargis, a fearless rider, as is Mystic, who is assessed as "a tough nut in a completely different way. He can jump big fences but his mind gets in the way.

"Caesar will either make or destroy you, or hang back and it is very difficult to stabilize him, get a level pace and yet maintain reasonable speed. When Caesar first came to Foxwood, he did not really want to try and did not balloon (bascule) in the air over jumps."

Broadway Joe, also a West Coast horse, is extremely excitable but possesses unlimited scope. "When you can get a tough horse like him to listen and he wins it gives enormous pleasure to all concerned with his training."

A horse like Patrick Butler's Mystic, who is clearly easily upset and afraid of having an accident, receives much confidence-building and responds far better to this than he would to rebuke. The aim is to ensure that he gets good schooling and ends feeling "like a tiger, not a mouse."

If a horse rears, Joe gets on. He is a real bronc rider, but also polished and smooth and if an occasion arises when a horse has to be punished, he can get the job done. If a horse tries to escape, he can control it with his long legs. He can contain lively horses with ease, and is better on an active jumper than a slug and, above all, has the vital desire to win.

"Girl riders are usually that degree more sensitive and certain horses get on better being kidded along rather than overpowered." One of Conrad's strengths is that he is capable of being as subtle as a girl, but if necessary can dominate and hold a horse in place as strongly as anyone. He is a natural horseman, completely lacking false pride; if a horse makes a mistake in the ring he is not embarrassed and would, for example, elect to go for three good strides coming out of a long combination rather than four, tripping and jabbing along.

"Both these riders analyze their horses and courses to the very last detail and part of their strength is that they are intelligent competitors."

In 1974, Canadian rider John Simpson brought his chestnut quarter-horse Texas, who is one of the world's outstanding natural jumpers, to Frances Rowe for six months. At the time, John had not a vast degree of international experience and Texas had begun stopping. "John is a person of great tenacity and perseverance and was very keen to learn and solve the problem." As it is some 2,940 miles from John's Calgary, Alberta home to Crozier, much of the subsequent communication has been by telephone, but has proved invaluable as the pair speak the same language and have established a real understanding of the difficulties faced. One direct result of this partnership was that in 1977 John and Texas made their first European trip a triumphant one. They were placed in every Grand Prix in which they competed, ending by winning the Rotterdam Grand Prix from a world-class field including such riders as former world champion David Broome, Harvey Smith and the 1977 European champion Johan Heins from Holland.

Frances' basic policy for the horses is that a top class performer will only remain there if he wants to jump and is comfortable doing so; therefore, soundness is of paramount importance. She is a firm adherent of whirlpool therapy, immersing the horses up to their knees and hocks – "a legacy of my racetrack days."

Every winter, the horses have a rest period when they get back to nature as much as possible; their shoes are removed and they are turned out to grass by day and brought in at night and allowed to grow fuzzy coats.

Although she says that being a female trainer in an exclusively man's world has proved an enjoyable experience, Frances' confident friendly manner hides the iron determination without which no trainer of either sex would reach this height. "I have certainly never felt at a disadvantage, and everyone concerned has always been most helpful."

Pauline Cushing

Groom

ONE OF THE MOST rewarding, interesting and demanding occupations concerned with the horse is that of the groom. Really good and dedicated grooms have the choice of a variety of posts all over the world. In just one week, the horseman's bible, the *Horse and Hound*, offered jobs in Switzerland, Teheran, Spain, France and the United States.

In Victorian times, this was entirely a male occupation and considered unseemly for a girl; but gradually, during the two World Wars, women began to come into stable work, and since 1945 the entire job has been revolutionized until, now at a show, there are usually 90 percent female grooms. The same applies to three day eventing and show-jumping.

Show-jumping offers perhaps the most exciting possibilities. Since the sport has recently developed so quickly on an international level and with a great increase of sponsorship in the 1960s and 1970s, there are now many opportunities to travel for the grooms of international jumpers. Such chances are keenly sought.

Britain's Pauline Cushing is right at the top of the tree, working for German rider Paul Schockemöhle who won an Olympic silver team medal riding Agent at the Montreal Games in 1976.

With fair hair, brilliant blue eyes and a friendly open face, Pauline stands out among the other grooms on the international show-jumping circuit, so it is no surprise to discover that the movie star Peter Cushing is her uncle. She is 5 feet 7 inches tall, strongly built, which is essential for the long

tiring hours and heavy work, with the fresh glowing complexion of someone who spends many hours in the open air.

When Pauline was a small girl, her parents farmed at Rush-
lake Green, in Sussex. By the time she was seven years old,
she had already begun to ride and showed great enthusiasm for
horses, so her parents gave their daughter her first pony. From
that moment, there was no stopping her. She began to compete
and win in local gymkhanas; saved her own pocket money to
buy a second larger pony and was soon winning at shows;
began jumping and hunting and became a member of the
East Sussex Pony Club.

By the time she was sixteen, Pauline began making young
horses, usually two- or three-year-olds, feeling her way on her
own with the instinct of a natural horseman. She began to
show-jump, and quite often rode at nearby Hickstead and
progressed sufficiently to ride in local point-to-points, finishing
second twice and third once. She had no basic instruction
other than at the Pony Club and learned much of what she
knows today by carefully watching experts with their horses
and talking with her friends and fellow competitors.

Initially, she kept her horses at home, and, in return, helped
her father twice a day with his herd of dairy cows. In 1970 her
parents moved into a cottage on the farm and her brother
moved into the main farmhouse and took over the full running
of the land. Pauline decided she would like to try her hand as a
full-time groom and spent a year with Marion Mould whom
she already knew a little as she had often competed on her
pony Gentle Lady against Marion and Stroller in junior
jumping classes.

A year later, she answered an advertisement in the *Horse
and Hound* and went to work for international show-jumper
Derek Ricketts at his father's yard at Quainton, near Ayles-
bury, in Buckinghamshire.

At the time, Derek, who is now one of Britain's leading
international riders and married to the 1976–1977 Champion
National Hunt jockey John Francome's sister Jill, was just
breaking into the international circuit. Pauline was responsible

Pauline Cushing with West German Olympic show-jump rider
Paul Schockemöhle at the World Championships at Aachen, 1978.
PHOTO: BOB LANGRISH

for six horses and now really began to understand more about
show-jumping at the top level. She was surprised and impressed to find how much Derek and his father thought of
their horses. At the shows she began spending a very great
deal of her time in the jumping pocket, the area between the
collecting ring and entrance, watching the different ways the
world's leading riders worked and so learning all the time.

The four years Pauline spent with the Ricketts were a happy
experience. The days were full and very tiring, and as Derek
became a regular member of the British team with the ill-fated
Beau Supreme, who was so tragically to break his off fore and
be put down at the Royal International Horse Show at

Wembley in July, 1975, there were regular trips to compete abroad.

After the excitement of journeys to Poland, Vienna, s'Hertogenbosch, Aachen and Geneva, Pauline began to comprehend at first hand the stresses and strains of long exhausting journeys and the problems encountered all too often at frontiers when traveling with horses.

Other horses in the Ricketts' stable at this time included the very consistent national horse Tyrolean Holiday, and Dakota, who was eventually sold to Holland, but who quickly became her favorite because he was so full of character. One of the most interesting journeys came in October–November 1973 when Derek was a member of the British team chosen to compete on the North American Fall Circuit along with David Broome, Harvey Smith, Graham Fletcher and Tony Newbery. This tour comprises three highly competitive indoor shows, Harrisburg or Washington, then on to New York and Toronto on the north shore of Lake Ontario in Canada for the Royal Winter Fair.

This is a month long tour and always hard for riders, horses and grooms alike for several reasons. They must cope with extremes of temperatures; on this occasion they were working in the seventies at the first show, and then only a fortnight later plunged into Arctic conditions at Toronto when the city experienced its first snowfall of the winter. Also, the competitions end late at night; for instance at Toronto that year on some nights the horses were often still jumping well after midnight. This means no respite with hardly any time to rest either at New York or Toronto because the many other show classes and national jumping competitions run during these two C.S.I.O's, meaning that exercising has to be done in shifts from 6.30 a.m. in the arena before the onset of the next morning's classes. (C.S.I.O. is an official international horse show where a Nations Cup is contested.)

In Toronto international show-jumpers are stabled upstairs in the permanent boxes and the public is allowed seemingly unlimited access to the stable area. The calm but firm good humor shown by Pauline and Davy Jones (David Broome's groom at that time) when they discovered some children about to feed Christmas trees to Beau Supreme and David's Manhattan, about thirty seconds after they had gone into the adjacent team tack room, is just another facet of the diplomacy and vigilance necessary when competing in unfamiliar surroundings in other countries.

By 1975, Pauline felt she needed a change and, as the British season ended after the Horse of the Year Show, was asked if she would like to go to Germany and work for Paul Schockemöhle. Her answer was yes. It would be a new challenge and seemed just the opportunity she was looking for.

Paul, the youngest of the three Schockemöhle brothers, lives at Mühlen, seventy kilometers north of Bremen in northern Germany. Working there was to prove very different from anything she had previously tackled. Paul's equestrian interests extend far beyond maintaining and riding a string of show-jumpers. He has approximately three hundred horses of his own, all of which are brought in during the long cold winter as the snow normally lies on the ground nonstop from November to March. There are usually about ten show jumpers, his current top two horses being Talisman, whom he rode in the individual show-jumping at Bromont, and Agent, with whom he was a member of the German silver medal winning team in the Prix des Nations. Others include speed horse Alcazar, and Lisander, who is a puissance specialist, and won at Emlohl and Dortmund in 1977 when he cleared 7 feet 2 inches.

There are always novice jumpers being brought on, a certain number for dealing purposes, mares and young stock; for Paul is very interested in breeding horses. Each winter there are about 100 weaned foals to be cared for; they are kept half in the main stable block and half in a large shed, three together in a box. One man is responsible for looking after the foals, but while Pauline is specifically in charge of the show-jumpers, she is not the kind of person to draw strict lines and fail to give a hand elsewhere if necessary.

A rare moment's relaxation for international groom Pauline Cushing (center), away from her charges. PHOTO: FINDLAY DAVIDSON

Pauline lives in a house away from the stables which she shares with two other girls. It is centrally heated, cleaned for them each day, and washing and drying machines and television are provided for them. On a typical day, Pauline gets up at 6.30 a.m., goes straight to the stables and feeds the horses. Then it is time for her own breakfast – usually just a cup of tea. She then mucks out, puts down fresh straw and is ready to ride out the first horse at 8.45. From then onward, she systematically works out and grooms each of the ten jumpers which she finds hard but pleasant work.

The facilities are excellent. Paul has made a time and motion study of the muck removal system and it has only to be moved a very short distance for collection, a vital point when caring for ten horses. There is a large covered school, a small hall for lunging and jumping, a big outdoor arena and plenty of land outside for boredom-relieving exercise and rides. The horses are usually finished and Pauline home between seven and eight in the evening when she has a hot bath, cooks her one substantial meal of the day and often reads a book for relaxation.

With her experience, Pauline has more responsibility than many grooms and certainly does more of the schooling because she has the knowledge to work the horses on the many occasions when their owner has not the time to do so himself.

Paul Schockemöhle has built up large business concerns quite apart from his not inconsiderable investment in horses. He has broiler chicken interests in Iran, which means he has to pay fairly regular visits there for periods of one to two weeks. He also has business concerns in the foods and equipment essential for the broiler industry and so relies heavily on Pauline for the well-being and preparation of his jumpers.

At shows, Pauline acts as groundsman and the pair work very much as a team. When Paul is at home, he always comes down to the stables at least once a day in his smokey blue Mercedes, and when he is away, no matter where, he always telephones Pauline daily to know how the horses are and if any problems have arisen.

The Montreal Games provided Pauline's first ever personal experience of the Olympics. She found the excitement and hospitality endless and everyone concerned far more friendly than she had imagined. One direct result of her travels round the world is that she has made many friends in different countries, which she finds happens quickly in the close world of horses where everyone involved shares the same major interest. The weeks she spent in Canada provided a splendid opportunity to see some of the friends she made in the United States on the British team tour with Derek Ricketts' horses in 1973.

Pauline is a top class groom because she is resourceful, responsible, experienced, dedicated, has a natural understanding of horses and is not afraid of the hard work inevitable with her job. For her the most rewarding times are when the horses go really well and win giving her a feeling of elation and making all her effort well worth while.

Elizabeth Broome

Equestrian Witness

"WHAT IS IT LIKE, being married to a super star?" Liz, wife of David Broome, one of the exclusive band of the world's top show-jumpers who spend ten months a year competing in international horse shows, was recently asked.

"I never think of him as a super star," she replied. "In fact, when I first went out to dinner with him on a double date with my brother Graham Fletcher and his wife Karen before they were married, I was pleasantly surprised to find that David seemed just like anyone else."

The May following this dinner, which had taken place during the Horse of the Year Show in 1975, the church bells pealed on a wet afternoon after David and Liz had been married in the parish church at Thirsk in Yorkshire.

A huge crowd of local farming, hunting and show-jumping friends from all over Britain then gathered for the reception which was held at the Fletchers' home at nearby Carlton Miniott. Graham's horses had a first-class view of the party as the marquee had been set up to incorporate their loose boxes, well garlanded in honor of the bridal couple.

Liz is the only daughter of hunting Yorkshire farmer Ken Fletcher. With her elder brother Graham quickly establishing himself as an international rider and her younger brother also riding, she soon found herself in the saddle. "I never learned to ride – ponies were just part of the family. I had to have a go because my father lashed the whip at me. I wasn't terribly good but I was never very ambitious. Men are more so. I competed in pony classes and then occasionally on horses in my late teens, but didn't feel I had what it really takes to get on.

"My best pony was a 12.2 h.h. filly called Twinkle Toes; then there was the 13.2 h.h. Flying Bus – he looked just like one too – and the 14.2 h.h. Irish Rock."

Despite this modest assessment Liz was quite often among the prize winners, and was simultaneously gathering first-hand knowledge of the show-jumping scene which was, although she little realized it, to stand her in good stead in later life.

It was a horse called The Likely Lad who finally helped Liz to the decision to give up show-jumping. "I had finished third on him in a Young Riders class, and after that every time I got home my father would say, 'How did you do, Elizabeth?' I told him I fell off so many times that in the end he started to say, 'Did you fall off today?' and that was when I finally decided to stop jumping."

Liz then trained at Leeds Secretarial College and took her first job there. Then followed another job in York, and later she worked from home for the Youth Club. After this she went to Canada with a girl friend and stayed with relations near Toronto. As they had no work permits they were unable to take jobs, but they made the most of their stay with the help of the Greyhound buses. "A fantastic tour in which we lived like gypsies" included seeing Ottawa, Montreal, Boston, New York, traveling down the eastern seaboard to Florida, Chattanooga, New Orleans, El Paso and San Antonio in Texas, Las Vegas, the Grand Canyon, San Diego, Los Angeles, Disneyland and San Francisco in California, up the western coast by the Pacific to Vancouver, and finally back over the Rockies to Toronto.

It was the journey of a lifetime, and when Liz arrived back in Yorkshire the time had come to take another job. She settled down right away from the show-jumping circuit, working as secretary to the bursar at Durham University.

In 1975 she took a few days off to go with her family to watch her brother Graham jump in the Horse of the Year Show at Wembley. The electric-paced indoor show where all the champions of the year are decided has a special air of nostalgia as goodbyes are said for the winter. This was where she first went out with her future husband.

After a holiday in Barbados the following February with Phil and Pauline Harris, who own many of the horses that David jumps, Liz and David decided to marry. The following May, after their marriage and a honeymoon in Scotland, Liz and David arrived back in Wales to make their home. They had planned to set up house in the grounds of Mount Ballan Manor where David's parents, Mr. and Mrs. Fred Broome, his sister Mary and his brother Fred Jr., all live. A bungalow which the grooms had once used at the other end of the stable yard seemed ideal, as they would be on their own but close at hand for David to work the horses with his father.

"What is a normal life?" reflected Liz. Then with a masterly understatement, "Well, I suppose my normal life wouldn't seem normal to most people." Housewives chained to a daily routine might be forgiven for imagining that Liz lives a life of luxury, floating from show to show on some exotic oriental magic carpet. It is true that in the space of a year she visits many exciting cities, such as Rome, Paris, Vienna, Berlin, Amsterdam and Brussels, but it is a very different role accompanying one of the world's top sportsmen as he competes to visiting such places on holiday.

"When I married I knew I wouldn't have a so-called normal life, and I didn't mind this because I have always found routine boring. On my holidays after I began work I still went to some shows with my brother Graham in order to help him, so I knew what kind of life I would have married to a professional show-jumper. What I had not realized was that David spends so much time abroad; he goes to far more international shows than Graham.

"One big difference about marrying and settling in Wales, which has made it not at all like being at home, is that I have left all my close friends behind, so I have no one in whom I can confide. In Wales no one thinks of me as Liz Fletcher; I am David Broome's wife, which is quite different, and of course I cannot betray confidences.

Elizabeth Broome at her wedding with her husband David (left) and her brother, Graham Fletcher.

"Loneliness is something I just have to cope with. Naturally I miss David being away about four days every week and most weekends. I plan my life round his horse shows because I have to. If he's away more than a fortnight I sometimes use the chance to go to Yorkshire and visit my family and friends. When I'm at home on my own the days pass quickly enough; it's in the evenings when I relax that I feel lonely.

"No two consecutive days of my life are ever the same. To other people's standards January is one of the quietest and most 'normal' months." At the very beginning there is the regular invitation to the Martell televised show-jumping meeting at Cindy Meade's Harwood Hall, Upminster, Essex.

David is one of the four joint Masters of the Curre Hunt, and January is one month when there is a slight lull in international jumping, so he can hunt with some regularity.

The first two weeks in February have become holiday time,

143

and are usually spent in Barbados in the West Indies. Phil and Pauline Harris are always there, and Frank Kernan from Northern Ireland, who has found some good horses for David, often brings his wife and children. Tennis is one sport which Liz and David enjoy playing together on holiday.

Then the season gets under way, and after the Lancia Championships at Park Hall Farm, Northwood, London, the journeying into Europe begins. In the spring of 1978 David went on to s'Hertogenbosch in Holland, Dortmund in Germany, and then Liz joined him at Gothenburg in Sweden. In alternate years there is then a major international show at Geneva, and then it is home to England for the Easter Hickstead Show and start of the British outdoor season.

More English shows are then on the schedule, because the prize money has increased so dramatically on the national circuit in recent years. Liz makes about eight trips a year to shows abroad, and goes as often as she can. She does not like to be away from home for long spells. If David is away for a month she usually tries to join him for a week. "Some shows abroad look after the riders' wives far better than others. There is of course a very great deal of sitting around, and time often hangs more heavily on a foreign show ground because you know so few people to talk to, compared with the English circuit.

"At a show I don't feel I do very much to help on the actual horse side because David usually has expert help available. For example I don't stand at the practice fence and try to give advice, but I'm always ready to hold the horses or fetch and carry. In the evening I try to help David to relax and unwind with a good meal and some time away from the horses."

The friendships that Liz has established since her marriage have tended to be with other wives who have been thrown into the same position. Derek Ricketts' wife Jill, Harvey Smith's wife Irene and her brother Graham's wife Karen have become good friends. Inevitably some of the wives and helpers talk of nothing but horses, but Liz and her friends enjoy discussing other interests too.

"David sometimes says to me that he thinks he is better off not having married a horsey person, that he finds it a form of relief to have a change of subject. When we drive home from a show I usually say how I think the horses went, but in our own home we rarely talk about horses. David has usually been concentrating on them for most of the day with his parents and sister Mary. I don't consciously create a change from horses – it just happens that way. I don't know enough to offer advice, all I can contribute is opinion from my level."

During a year David is away for six to eight months, and at these times she has become a regular helper with the vast load of secretarial work associated with the series of Wales and West shows which the Broome family have established on their permanent showground, Mount Ballan Manor.

Turning around between shows is a busy time. The caravan has to be cleaned and repacked with food for the next few days. There are a score of little jobs, such as washing breeches and going to the dry cleaners for red coats, which Liz has to manage in the short time before the Broome horses and their rider are on the road again. Liz makes practical use of her secretarial training to deal with David's office work, handling his considerable mail and helping with his books.

"When I see him on television I don't think of him as a star but as a person I know. I would much rather he was ordinary, just as when we first met I thought how normal he was. If I worried about his falling off and getting hurt I would be frightened all the time and never watch him jump. When I do watch I am thinking how the horse is going. I don't see every fence as a disaster and don't think about falls. It's not like steeplechasing where a rider could be killed or paralyzed for life."

When I talked to her, Liz was much looking forward to the arrival of her first baby, James, who was born in August 1978. As soon as she feels fully fit she plans to take her child to as many shows as possible. "We were married so that we could be together and I hope it will be possible that we all three travel around most of the English shows."

Ruth McMullen

Exhibitor

RUTH MCMULLEN is the only woman who competes with
and indeed regularly beats the men in the world of professional
showing. This is a tough school requiring many hours of
painstaking skill and patience to gild the ugly duckling into a
swan. A champion show hunter is of increasing value, with the
ringside and collecting ring a market place for event horses,
show-jumpers and sometimes chasers, as well as horses for the
hunting field. Few horses possess perfect conformation,
action and temperament. The art of showing is to make the
animal in question seem as correct and attractive as possible
in appearance, with first-class manners and smooth ride.

Ruth's parents were not horse oriented, though one of her
father's first cousins was the millionaire Paul Mellon, who has
one of the finest collections in the world of sporting art at his
Virginia home, and who has owned so many first-class race
horses, among them Mill Reef who won the Derby in 1971.
Her first rides were on a local carthorse near her home in
Cheshire, England. She cycled seven miles each way to a riding
school for lessons. Then, eventually, by carrying out errands
for her parents, she and her brother managed to save £27 to
buy their first pony.

"This was my initiation into dealing. The pony, Smokey,
who was Welsh, had been sold as a four-year-old. We soon
discovered that he was only two and had been gelded just
the week before. He didn't get me off but I found it very hard
to get the saddle on at first!"

The next pony in a series that followed was Peggy, "A fat

Ruth McMullen on Lady Aubrey Buxton's Champion Middleweight hunter Crown Court. PHOTO: DAVID GUIVER

round black mixture," but all the time Ruth was acquiring valuable experience and winning hundreds of rosettes in gymkhanas and junior jumping classes.

When her grandfather died, he left Ruth, her sister and brother a yacht, which they immediately sold to buy a jumping pony. "We bought a gray Connemara mare that Joe Makin of the famous Yorkshire show-jumping family had brought over from Ireland."

Her name was Crescendo, and after the pair had progressed to Grade J.A. and Ruth was out of junior classes, they used her to breed. Her offspring were all by premium stallions and very successful. The first, Court Calypso by Court Nez, won the Riding Clubs Dressage and Horse Trials Championships. Another was Court Calando by Starlata, who became the leading Junior Jumper of the year in 1971. Court Cadenza became a Grade A show-jumper in only a year with international show-jumper Derek Ricketts.

Ruth has never liked selling horses, and so, after leaving school, she started to give lessons to help pay for her horses.

Her first small riding school was in Lancashire, and then in 1953 she moved to Hertfordshire with her parents. At first she had another riding school, but later concentrated on showing and her three novice jumpers, who included Court Calypso who jumped so well.

Before she settled at her present home in Norfolk, she had help at various times from Captain Edy Goldman, show-jumping training from the late Colonel Jack Talbot-Ponsonby and Seamus Hayes, and more recently from Dick Stillwell. "He is great on flat work and very helpful whatever I am aiming at. I responded immediately to his method of teaching, enjoyed working with him, and whatever my aim has been at the time I have always learned so much from him."

In 1966, when the stables which she was renting were sold for building, she moved to Norfolk which had always been one of her favorite counties.

Mr. and Mrs. Crawford invited her to move to their home at Carbrooke, some twenty miles south-west of Norwich, and converted their extensive stable yard for her; she now has seventeen boxes there. She does not do livery work and concentrates solely on breaking, schooling, showing and teaching clients who bring their own horses.

"I like all my horses to do more than one thing," she commented, and this is shown by the fact that she prepares horses for eventing and show-jumping as well as the show ring, and that the variety of work her horses carry out prevents them from ever showing any signs of the boredom so prevalent in the show-ring today.

One of the first horses she was asked to produce was a potentially high class hack called Clearway, who had been discovered by top showman and former international show-jumper David Barker and belonged to Mr. Pike. "He was a naughty horse. I learned a lot from him and gained confidence when he finished second at the Royal Richmond Horse Show, and won the Riding Clubs Dressage Championship the year before Calypso. He did very well at county level."

It was when Mr. Bill Ransom, who was Master of the Blankney Hounds at the time, asked her to show a brown thoroughbred called Brother Bill that she first hit the real headlines. He arrived as an average two-year-old and went on to score at such estimable shows as Royal Windsor and British Timken. Quite typically Ruth expected him to prove his worth in other fields, and before his competitive days were over he had won at the Royal Norfolk in a working hunter class and also taken a section of the Fenton Horse Trials.

"Paul Rackham, who had seen me ride on Brother Bill, then offered me Heron's Phase, and this was to prove the turning point in my showing career. He was a bay, an Irish lightweight by Dark Heron, and had yet again been found by David Barker, who had purchased him from the late Tom Dreaper, trainer of the immortal Arkle."

Ruth's successes with Heron's Phase, high class and hard to fault but a problematical horse, were legion. Simultaneously she was teaching Mr. Rackham's children at his stables twenty-five miles away, and buying them a suitable string of ponies.

1976, Ruth McMullen is voted winner of the Martini Trophy which is organized by Light Horse and Pony *magazine, for the leading leading show representatives.* PHOTO: STEPHEN AUSTIN NEWSPAPERS LTD.

A series of winners followed, among them Game Moss by the multi-winning premium stallion Game Rights, who was bred in the heart of the Duke of Beaufort's hunt by his heir, Mr. David Somerset, and broken by no less than Olympic three day event gold medallist Colonel Frank Weldon. "He was another difficult horse, but I enjoy a challenge and I like bringing out new horses or transforming those I find down the line rather than the prospect of taking over champions."

At this time Allister Hood, who went on to take the Show Hunter of the Year title on Mr. Rackham's Langton Orchid in 1975, was working with Ruth and learning much of his present expertise – a fact which he readily acknowledges.

When Lady Zinnia Pollock, whose attentions have ranged from top class show-jumpers to an exclusive and successful London boutique, transferred her interest to the show hunter world, she was quick to enlist Ruth's help.

In 1975 the late premium stallion, Little Cloud's son Picture Play, won the Windsor Championship. Another premium stallion horse, Prince Crispin, by Charlie Mumford's Crespin Rouge, was continually in the money in middleweight classes, and Peacemaker was champion at the Royal Norfolk Show. Mrs. Campbell's Billet continued in winning vein, finishing second at the Horse of the Year Show.

Others who won consistently included Mr. Fenwick's lightweight Fieldmaster, who is now so consistent in the show-jumping arena with Caroline Bradley, and Valentine. Ruth's exploitation of Valentine's outstanding floating action made him a superlative four-year-old – an age at which he was most frequently shown by Allister Hood.

In 1977 and 1978 the chestnut middleweight Crown Court was her top exhibit. Owned by the naturalist Lord Aubrey Buxton and his wife, he has the elusive charisma essential to the top show horse.

Right now she aims not to enlarge her establishment. "What I enjoy is giving the personal touch. At the moment I have an excellent head girl, Brigid Ensten, and usually two working pupils, and that's big enough."

She has also derived enormous pleasure from training the West Norfolk Pony Club team who won the Pony Club Championship in 1970.

Ruth commands the highest respect from her fellow men professionals. Exceptionally hard working and unassuming, she carries out a demanding eight-month show program which would daunt lesser mortals.

"The hunter people," she reflected, "are a really good bunch. My aim is individual attention rather than turning out horses off a conveyor belt. I don't often sell horses because I *can't* sell them – I like them too much. I am very happy that I now have a part share in Crown Court. He is learning to jump in preparation for working hunter classes. Another interest makes all the difference to show horses. It means that they don't go round like clockwork, but wonder what's coming next and where the next jump or challenge is."

Ruth McMullen is thorough and painstaking and schools her horses carefully so that they are well balanced from the correct center of gravity rather than precariously on the forehand. Proof of her diligence in dealing with individual horses is that even now, as an established star, she is not too proud to go back to Dick Stillwell when she has a problem and needs help. He spares no punches and was especially helpful with Billet, one of the most volatile horses which she has had to date. This special care for each horse means that Ruth McMullen will be a feature of the British show ring for as long as she cares to compete.

Elspeth Ferguson

Pony Breeder

NESTLING ON THE SIDE OF the gentle orchard-covered slopes of Fladbury Hill, half-way between Evesham and Pershore, lies Miss Elspeth Ferguson's Rose Vean Riding Pony Stud. It is one of the world's specialist studs and its ponies are of such caliber that they are in constant demand in many countries. There is special interest shown by breeders and exhibitors in the United States, Australia and New Zealand, and in Europe, particularly in Holland and Germany.

Miss Ferguson's father was a Scot and her mother English. When she was a child, the family divided their time between Newton Stewart in Galloway and Hindlip near Worcester. Although her parents were not interested in horses, her uncle and grandfather gave her backing and understood her wish to breed ponies. She soon learned to ride, hunted with the Croome, and during the war worked on a farm at nearby Eckington. On this farm, she was fascinated by the Shetland stallion and small mares. Then, when her father died soon after the war and his herd of Guernseys was sold, for the first time there was room at home to breed ponies.

She began with Shetlands and, blessed with the essential eye for a horse, the awareness that to reach the top there is no room for sentimentality, and a shrewd business head, she had soon begun to achieve the first of a series of what are by now thousands of victories.

In 1952, the Royal Show, which traveled around England at the time, was held at Newton Abbott in Devon. Miss Ferguson spent some considerable time talking to Miss

Calmady-Hamlyn, the renowned breeder of Dartmoor ponies, who did much to preserve the breed during World War II. Their ponies were in adjacent boxes and before they left the showground Miss Calmady-Hamlyn said she would shortly be sending up a Dartmoor mare to Miss Ferguson's Stud. Miss Ferguson explained that she could not afford one, only to be told, "I am not asking you to pay. This is a present."

Thus Miss Ferguson also began to breed Dartmoors, experiencing success for a number of years. Janus, a top class stallion, was another gift from Miss Calmady-Hamlyn. She still has a mare with some Dartmoor blood, Rosevean Peewit, who produced 1976 Lloyds Bank Champion Rosevean Eagles Hill's first ever foal in 1977. Miss Ferguson backed her own judgment when she spotted and bought Peewit's dam in the unlikely surroundings of Gloucester market.

By 1959, Miss Ferguson had been so successful that she was now in a position to change to riding ponies, which had for long been her aim.

She was fortunate to acquire the stallion Bwlch Zephyr who, with his father, Bwlch Valentino, and son, Bwlch Hill Wind, has proved one of the greatest influences on the riding ponies of the post-war era. He proved to be an immeasurable asset. Miss Ferguson had been responsible for showing Zephyr's dam, Miss Minette, under saddle for her owner, Mrs. Nell Pennell, during her outstanding show career and Mrs. Pennell had always promised her one of "Miny's children." When Miss Minette's gray son, Bwlch Zephyr, was one year old, he was a gangly and naughty colt. His habit of hunting calves and chasing sheep had made his owner decide it would be a good idea to have him gelded. It was then arranged that Miss Ferguson should have him for a season and show him for his owner. At the end of the year, Miss Ferguson was able to buy him, to a degree unwittingly assuring the errant colt's future as one of the great riding pony foundation stallions.

Zephyr's son, Bwlch Hill Wind, out of Criban Red Heather, a Welsh Section B foundation stock mare, also sired many exceptional ponies until his comparatively early end in August

Elspeth Ferguson with the immortal foundation stallion, Bwlch Zephyr. PHOTO: BERROW'S NEWSPAPERS

1977 at the age of fourteen. Hill Wind, who had been turned out in a field, damaged a tendon in a hind leg and went right down on it. When, despite expert veterinary attention and a remedial high heeled shoe, it was apparent that he would not be able to lead a normal life again, like all true lovers of horses, Miss Ferguson took the very difficult decision to end his days.

Other stallions owned by Miss Ferguson include Erimus Morning Star (1972), bred by Vanessa de Quincey, by Zephyr from her former show hack Kalya, a winner three times at the Royal Show and twice champion at the West Midlands Stallion Show, and Rosevean Eagles Hill. Eagles Hill's excellence was recognized when he won the Lloyds Bank Championship as a yearling in 1976 and then again in 1978. This championship is open to all breeds of horses and ponies shown in hand. The larger exhibits, such as three-year-old hunters tend to have an advantage, and it was quite exceptional for a pony yearling to be victorious.

Eagles Hill is the result of an alliance between the best of Miss Ferguson's blood lines. He is by Bwlch Hill Wind out of her remarkable foundation mare Perdita, who was twenty-one when he was foaled. Perdita is an Anglo-Arab standing 14.1½ h.h. who was left to his present owner by Mrs. Hunt. She is by Count d'Orsay out of Maid of the Morning, who is by Umidwar, and every foal she produced has been a champion. She herself is the only mare to have been champion on three occasions at the Ponies of Britain Show

Because of his dam's age, Eagles Hill was not shown as a foal, but was unbeaten as a yearling when he was unusually mature, winning seventeen firsts and twenty-two championships. He had his first mares as a two-year-old, a season in which he was only lightly shown but beat Mrs. Mansfield's Rotherwood Peep Show at the Royal and was Young Stock Champion at the National Pony Show. At a time when there is a trend for light-boned show ponies, Eagles Hill has an abundance of flat bone and it is to be hoped that the attractive dark gray has a promising crop of foals and becomes a fashionable pony stallion.

Merry Mountain (1972), a very dark chestnut whose grandsire was the racehorse Precipitation, has splendid limbs, stands 12.2 h.h. and is line bred to Zephyr, being by Bwlch Hill Wind out of Chuckle, a full sister to the late champion riding pony mare, Mirth. Chuckle and Mirth were by Zephyr out of Promise.

Trout Stream (1976) was bred in conjunction with the late Lt. Col. Edward Williams-Wynn, who owned the famous Coed Coch Stud, for whom Miss Ferguson always showed several ponies until his untimely death in 1977. Trout Stream is by Coed Coch Hillstream, who is by Hill Wind, out of a mare by Zephyr who goes back to Vilmorin on her dam's side and is almost white in color with an unusual black mane and tail, just like Vilmorin.

Another mare is Perdita's sister, Maid of the Mountains, also out of Maid of the Morning and who looks straight thoroughbred but is by the Welsh pony, Coed Coch Berwynfa.

Robert Gilbert, a Scot from Edinburgh, has been the Rosevean stud groom for a decade. The resident ponies usually number about forty and he has four assistant grooms to help look after them. The friendly manner with which the ponies greet visitors and well-kept boxes and yards are indicative of his first-class management.

In January 1974, Miss Ferguson decided to move to Fladbury Hill from Hindlip because the coming of the M5 Motorway had made for masses of new building closing in around the stud.

There are forty acres at Fladbury Hill, some of which have been cleared of apple trees, with a few left to provide shade. The land, in the center of the Vale of Evesham fruit growing and market gardening country, is considered some of the best in the area. A bulldozer carved out a sheltered niche in the side of the hill where the compact stables are grouped and sheltered from the worst of the wind. Two covered barns were brought from Hindlip and are divided into approximately thirty individual pens for some of the mares and youngsters, who usually number about fifteen They can quickly be converted into a covered school area so the ponies can exercise themselves indoors if there is prolonged severe weather.

At Fladbury Hill, Miss Ferguson has not only some of the world's best ponies but a most magnificent view. From her house she can look down over her fields, which fall to the Evesham-Pershore Road, south to the soft slopes of Bredon Hill, where she rents a further forty acres of land and grazes some of the ponies from September until January each year, then south-west across the Worcestershire plain to the huge purple mass of the Malvern Hills.

Mrs. Philip Fleming

Polo Player

"IT WAS ALWAYS so much more fun playing against the men than the women," Mrs. Philip Fleming reminisced. She played polo over a period spanning five decades until she finally retired in 1970 from the game that gave her so much pleasure, but still maintains a very active equestrian life, enjoying three days hunting a week during the season, making and showing hacks and ponies and driving.

Born Joan Hunloke, she was brought up by her parents Sir Philip and Lady Hunloke at Wingerworth Hall, near Chesterfield in Derbyshire. Sir Philip was groom-in-waiting to George V and her mother a fine horsewoman and judge who showed many top class riding and driving horses and also kept Shetland ponies.

From a tiny child onward, Mrs. Fleming always rode, and she had a compulsive interest in riding from this time on. She rode most of her mother's ponies in the show ring. Her very first outing was at Bicester Horse Show when she was six years old and both she and her sister, Lady Paynter, rode little white ponies. Lady Paynter was quite a few years older so more dashing at the gallop. Mrs. Fleming shouted to her to stop, but luckily the famous family stud groom, Simpkin, rushed out and caught her as she lost control.

As Joan grew up she became a keen cricketer and played for the very distinguished White Heather Ladies Team and also, by way of contrast, looked after her father's herd of Dexter cows. She transferred to hacks, and it must constitute something of a record that some half a century later she won

Mrs. Philip Fleming (left) avoids a pile-up playing polo at Roehampton in 1947. Billy Walsh (right) is less fortunate.
PHOTO: SPORT AND GENERAL

the Small Hack Class with a degree of aplomb and elegance at the Leicestershire County Show in 1978 on Wingerworth Sassenach. Then polo became a passion, and now as a septuagenerian she is still a regular winner in the show hack, mountain and moorland pony and driving pony fields.

Her interest in polo was aroused early when she watched her uncle, Godfrey Heseltine, playing polo. He schooled ponies to a high level and then sold them to the Indians. Then, when in the early 1920s she married Philip Fleming, they first lived at Grendon Hall at Grendon Underwood in Oxfordshire, where Sir John Peyton, who lived at Swift's House, near Bicester, soon came and called to see if her husband would like to start the Kirtlington Polo Club.

Mrs. Fleming had a roan pony that seemed suitable; she acquired some sticks and began practicing at home, often using the polo pit. In its simplest form a polo pit is a pit dug into the ground with a flat center on which there is a wooden horse wearing a saddle.

159

She never had any lessons but everyone she met who played helped by telling her how to play. An early problem was learning not to wang the pony's legs with her stick.

A note she made in the polo manual she used at the time reads:

The Four Fundamental Strokes:
Off Side Forehander.
Off Side Backhander.
Near Side Forehander.
Near Side Backhander.
Three others – the drive, the pull and the cut.
Follow through, keep your eye on the ball, head down.

The polo bug had bitten and by the time she was thirty-three, Mrs. Fleming gave up her showing, show-jumping and driving, although she was now an experienced whip and had figured among the prize winners at the Royal Richmond Horse Show on more than one occasion, in order to concentrate on the game.

"I just grew keener and keener and keener and gradually had the chance to play on every known ground. I was quite furious when the war came and I had to join the W.A.A.F.'s and it all ended for a time."

By the early 1950s, with the war over, the Flemings had moved to Mrs. Fleming's present home, Barton Abbey at Steeple Aston in Oxfordshire. Polo was gradually resumed and she was once again able to play regularly, usually for Kirtlington Park or their own Barton Abbey team with its well-known blue and yellow colors.

The polo ground is 300 yards long, 160 yards wide if boarded, or 200 yards wide if unboarded with goal posts eight yards apart. A full game consists of eight chukkers but usually four are played.

Each player is handicapped from minus two up to ten goals (the best players). A team consists of four players and the aggregate handicap of the four players is the team handicap.

The game is very demanding on the ponies so they normally play only two chukkers in an afternoon with a rest of at least one chukker in between.

The polo pony has to be able to turn on the proverbial sixpence, twist his hocks, be as handy as a cat, able to accelerate with the rapidity of the quarter horse and, above all, be brave. "It is not unusual for them to be hit between the eyes by a ball but they always carry on. I like a pony of quality, a good mouth is important and they must gallop. I prefer not too long a neck so you can hit underneath it. Nowadays the ponies are mostly thoroughbreds but they used to be all 14.2 h.h. ponies. The Argentine ponies were usually very well trained and easy to play. In the 1930s, they could be purchased for about £400 but I'm afraid £4,000 to £5,000 is about the mark now," Mrs. Fleming told me.

Polo boots are vital to protect the ponies' fetlocks and cannon bones from blows from both ball and stick. The stick, most usually with a cigar-shaped head weighing $6-7\frac{1}{2}$ ounces, and a bamboo shaft, is whippy and can be very dangerous if it misses its target.

The players too get involved in some nasty accidents. Mrs. Fleming recalled, "Once I broke my nose and I think it was my own fault. I put my stick through the pony's legs, sailed on and fell onto my hat. You do get the most hideous blows especially if you don't wear knee caps. Once at Ranelagh, which was one of the most famous London grounds, I had the most vicious whack on my knee which remained purply-black for weeks. After that I always wore knee caps."

On another occasion, she was involved in a head-on collision which resulted in both ponies limping away on three legs. "The veterinary surgeon said they would both have to be shot. I was severely concussed, I had double vision for nine months and wore a patch over one eye, but it gradually disappeared. I'm glad to say the ponies did not have to be shot."

Lady Hunloke had a house in Somerset, The Firs at Porlock, and once when she was staying there Mrs. Fleming saw a team of ladies playing sidesaddle against a rather indifferent

Barton Abbey Team. Mrs. Philip Fleming (second from right) on Oakapple and right, Wing Commander Alan Roberts.
PHOTO: SPORT AND GENERAL

men's team. The ladies team proved to contain some surprises as the riders included Lady Chesham and Mrs. Maurice Kingscote while another turned out to be a well-known high handicap player, Stanley Barton, masquerading as a woman with a wig and dividing skirt. The sidesaddle team won hands down.

Before World War II the members of the leisured society who had the means and the time to play the game as it should be played enjoyed matches at Hillmorton, a marvelous ground at Rugby which no longer exists, Cowdray in Sussex, Cirencester in Gloucestershire and Ranelagh and Roehampton in London.

In the late 1940s, when a changing social and political scene irrevocably altered the pattern of life, clubs had not yet developed and few men were able to play polo regularly. This was the time when the women really came into their own and men's teams were happy to have a good woman on their side.

Ladies' matches were not regular events but some did take place. Mrs. Fleming told me, "I far preferred playing with the men because the ladies were often inclined to get into the middle of the field and scratch about together. In a game with men, you could usually depend on the back really hitting the ball, opening up the game and keeping it on the move. I was lucky to play largely in men's games, and with good men."

Mrs. Fleming played from a handicap of 0. Handicaps start at −2, and her standard was only achieved by two other women in the 1970s.

Games did take place between ladies' teams. One was at Kirtlington Park on July 19, 1958. Mrs. Fleming wore the red-and-gray Number 3 shirt for Kirtlington Park, and together with Mrs. R. A. Budgett, Miss E. Colquhoun and Mrs. Worsley beat Miss Judy Forwood, Mrs. H. Forbes, Miss T. P. Walsh and Miss Lucas, who were representing Woolmers Park, by 5–2 goals.

Mrs. Fleming considered her two best ponies were La Linda, which she bought from the famous Balding family after playing at Rugby just after the war, and Oakapple who belonged to Dick Hobson. Oakapple had been lent as a hack to Mrs. Duggie Stuart, then Phoebe Gosling who lived at Stratton Audley. In 1949, Mrs. Fleming was chosen to play for Henley in the Cowdray Cup at Goodwood and at the last moment one of her ponies went lame. In desperation she rang Phoebe Gosling to ask for the loan of Oakapple, who was turned out in the field, and hadn't been on a polo field for some time. However, he played marvelously and remained with Mrs. Fleming to the end of his days.

The Henley team consisted of Mrs. Fleming, Squadron Leader Roberts (whose daughter Lavinia Black is one of the best women players in the 1970s), Captain Johnnie Butler and Billy Walsh.

This proved to be a great day as Henley reached the finals, where they beat a Cotswold team consisting of Mrs. A. Gibb,

A. Gibb, H. Freeborn and M. Holden-White by $5\frac{1}{2}$ goals to 2.

The Times polo correspondent reported: "Henley beat Cotswold in the final tie by $5\frac{1}{2}$ goals to 2 and thoroughly deserved their victory. Though they received a start of $2\frac{1}{2}$ goals, they managed to hold their opponents for three chukkas, and in the last were certainly in winning vein. There must have been between 3,000 and 4,000 spectators on the ground and as Cowdray itself was out, every one rather hoped that Henley might win, for they have not had the best of luck in the past two years. But the start suggested that an old tale would repeat itself and that Henley would again fail to settle down, for Cotswold got 2 goals in the first chukka, both by Lieutenant Freeborn, and the first by a remarkable shot under his pony.

"Butler, with two of Major David's best ponies to ride, however, was a tower of strength, and he set Mrs. Fleming away on a great run on her bay mare La Linda to score an excellent goal. Holden White playing a dun Argentine, sent a terrific shot – Americans, unlike ourselves, learn to hit a polo ball early in life – but it just went wide. On the whole, however, Cotswold were keeping the initiative and were mostly in their opponents' half of the ground in the rather slow third chukka, when the game seldom opened out and there was a good deal of missing.

"All this time Walsh had been playing impeccably at back for Henley, but in the final chukka he and Easter Morn excelled themselves. First he caught, and took out Freeborn on the Cowdray chestnut Cheltenham; next he sent Mrs. Fleming away on Oakapple, followed up and netted a hard shot through the Cotswold goal for $4\frac{1}{2}$–2 and almost certain victory. Just before the final bell he added another."

The game of polo is extremely exhausting and demanding. Half an hour's play galloping full out is the equivalent of a half hour game of squash. So it is plain to see why women in England were rarely included in any polo matches until their gradual emancipation and subsequent opportunities to take part in more active sports.

The Queen

Breeder and Owner of Thoroughbreds

JUDGING BY THE WAY the Queen's face lights up with interest whenever she is present at any sporting event involving horses, and her obvious spontaneous happiness when she is photographed riding, there is no doubt that she derives great pleasure from horses.

This is no surprise. With very few exceptions British monarchs have all been genuinely interested in racing. It was Queen Anne who founded Ascot but the Queen has surpassed her ancestors with the position she now holds as one of the leading British racehorse owners and breeders of thoroughbreds.

Her racehorses are her personal, very private and much enjoyed hobby, and one about which she is extremely knowledgeable. Since her accession to the throne in 1952 she has been more successful than any other private owner, with the possible exceptions of Jim Joel, who is now an octogenarian, and the very different and internationally based Sangster partnership.

Broadly speaking, the Queen's horses are divided into two main departments: the Royal Racing Establishment where horses are bred for racing; and the Royal Mews, which comes under the control of the Master of the Horse. This important office was filled by the Duke of Beaufort for forty-two years until he retired in 1978 having also earned himself a special role in British equestrian history as the founder of Badminton Horse Trials and Master of the Beaufort Hounds. On his retirement he was succeeded by the Earl of Westmoreland.

The Crown Equerry is Colonel Sir John Miller, who oversees as wide a range of horses as any in the world. These include the State horses, the carriage horses, grays and the bay carriage horses – all royal horses, in fact, other than racehorses and the thoroughbred breeding stock. In the early part of Queen Victoria's reign, the main carriages were pulled by cream horses but they were succeeded by the now famous Windsor grays. They pull the Coronation Coach, the coach used to open Parliament and leading Ascot carriages. The back-up carriages are now pulled by bays, often Cleveland Bays and some German Oldenburgers or part-bred horses. Colonel Sir John Miller has overall responsibility for the private riding horses, hacks, event horses (such as the Queen's Goodwill, who was Princess Anne's 1976 Montreal Olympic partner, and Countryman III who was a member of Britain's Olympic gold medal three-day event team at Stockholm in 1956 when ridden by Bertie Hill), Prince Philip's carriage horses and Prince Charles' hunters and polo ponies. The Royal Mews is also responsible for the well-being of the occasional gifts of different breeds of horses the Queen receives from all over the world. Another well-known Royal Mews inmate at Windsor is Burmese, the mare presented by the Royal Canadian Mounties some years ago and ridden by the Queen at the Trooping of the Color ceremony ever since, and ridden by Her Majesty at weekends.

The Queen had already enjoyed some of the thrills of owning a racehorse when she shared the steeplechaser Monaveen with her mother. She had always had a keen interest in flat racing and even as a child looked forward with enthusiasm to visiting the late Fred Darling's stables at Beckhampton with her father, King George VI.

When Queen Elizabeth II came to the throne on her father's death in 1952, Aureole, by Hyperion out of Angelola, a daughter of the superb foundation mare Feola, who cost 3,000 guineas in 1934 as a yearling, was two years old. Feola was twice placed in the Classics. Her daughter Hypericum and great granddaughter Highclere both won the One Thou-

Ascot, 1977. The Queen in the winners' enclosure with her horse, Duke of Normandy, after it won the Fenwolf Stakes.
PHOTO: R. BOND

sand Guineas. Hypericum gave the Queen one of her earliest racing excitements when the filly bolted into the car park on the way to the start before her win in the Guineas. On the male line, she also made her mark on the world's top blood lines. As well as Aureole, her descendants include Vaguely Noble, St. Paddy, St. Crespin III, Vienna, Round Table and Baldric.

Aureole was brilliant but had the excitable temperament that very often goes with a bright chestnut coat. Because of this, for a long time it seemed likely that his exceptional ability would not be realized. In his Derby year, 1953, he had the misfortune to finish second to Sir Victor Sassoon's Pinza. The following year he came into his own as a four-year-old, helped enormously by the patience and understanding of the

167

royal trainer, the late Captain Sir Cecil Boyd-Rochford and jockey Eph Smith. He won four races including the Coronation Cup, the Hardwicke Stakes and the King George VI and Queen Elizabeth Stakes, named after the Queen's parents.

This final victory confirmed him as a top class international performer and also the success of Feola's family. Aureole, who died in 1974, became one of Feola's most renowned grandsons. He was the champion British sire in 1960 and 1961 and sired leading sires. He was apparently a very independent and naughty character and often got loose in training at Newmarket, as indeed he did before adding the King George VI and Queen Elizabeth Stakes to his triumphs.

Captain Charles Moore, who had been appointed manager of the Royal Studs in 1937, leaned toward staying blood, especially from the lines of Gainsborough and Swynford. It was from Captain Moore that the Queen acquired much of her now profound knowledge of pedigrees and thoroughbreds and Aureole's final triumph must have been all that was necessary to further kindle an already deep interest in the turf.

The Queen's interest had been initially aroused during the war when her father took her down to Beckhampton to see Big Game and Sun Chariot, which he had leased from the National Stud. She had never seen thoroughbreds working before and afterward, as she patted them in their stables, she had the wonderful experience of feeling the satiny softness of a thoroughbred for the first time.

Since 1952 she has won well over three hundred races with horses she has bred herself – an especially remarkable achievement because she seldom has more than just over twenty horses at the Royal Studs, a mere drop in the ocean when compared to such studs as the vast Wildenstein racing empire, which is based in France and has ramifications in the United States and Great Britain, and Bunker Hunt's international complex.

For some years she had her yearling fillies broken in at home at Windsor, finding, like so many other true horsemen and women, that this is one of the most interesting parts of breeding horses and the ideal time to assess their temperament, character and movement and see exactly how they are likely to develop in the future.

The Queen does not normally buy yearlings, unless it is to create a new family. Once, however, years ago she went to the Doncaster Sales with Captain Charles Moore and Lord Porchester, now her Racing Manager, and fell in love with a filly, Stroma, who was to be the dam of Canisbay, who won the Eclipse Stakes for her.

Stroma, a relatively inexpensive purchase, was also to turn out to be the grand dam of Dunfermline, the Queen's double classic winner in her Jubilee Year. When Mr. Joel and the other owners of Royal Palace gave her a nomination, she decided to send Stroma to him. It was clearly a good match on paper but she felt that from the point of view of conformation it was also desirable and was proved so right as the outcome was the filly Dunfermline.

Feola's grandson, Aureole, helped his owner to become leading owner for the first time in 1954. Two decades later, the Queen's great filly Highclere, Feola's great-granddaughter, won the One Thousand Guineas and the French Oaks and a year later ran second in the King George VI and Queen Elizabeth Stakes. She was trained by Major Dick Hern at West Ilsley in Berkshire. In 1978 the Queen had three trainers: Dick Hern, whose stables are owned by Sir Michael Sobell; Ian Balding at Kingsclere due south of Newbury; and William Hastings Bass at Newmarket.

Her Majesty likes to make regular visits to her trainers. When she arrives, she looks around and closely inspects each animal in its stable. Then she goes up to the gallops and sees her horses work in groups.

Ian Balding's Kingsclere Stables trained the filly Escorial to win the Musidora Stakes in 1974. Since then he has trained the Queen's Joking Apart who was third in the 1975 One Thousand Guineas and in 1978 produced a bay-brown foal by Vaguely Noble.

Like any other owner, the Queen expects her horses to pay

Epsom, 1977. The Queen arrives on Derby Day with Lord Halifax.
PHOTO: SPORT AND GENERAL

their way. Fittingly 1977, Jubilee Year, was to prove Dunfermline's year. The Queen watched the Oaks on television because Prince Andrew returned that day from Canada, but the excitement in the Royal viewing party must have been intense as Dunfermline suddenly accelerated a quarter of a mile out. Very aptly Willie Carson celebrated his first season with Dick Hern in the Jubilee Year by heading Freeze the Secret by the time they crossed the line.

It is sad that the Queen misses many opportunities to enjoy seeing her best horses triumph in major races. Prior to 1977 only four fillies this century had won both the Oaks and St. Leger. At Doncaster in September 1977 the Queen was not present but the question: Could Dunfermline give her a Jubilee double? was uppermost in every racegoer's mind.

Dunfermline's owner was at Balmoral at the time where the Prime Minister, Mr. James Callaghan, was staying for the weekend, and so again she was forced to watch on television. She had two runners and Alan Bond did a first-class job on Gregarious as pacemaker. When Willie Carson and Dunfermline reached the straight, she had to overcome Lester Piggott and Alleged, who were unbeaten in five races, but Dunfermline strengthened to win and the Queen's experience and knowledge were rewarded with the winning of two Classics in one year. Dunfermline could not have selected a better year than Jubilee Year to become only the fifth filly this century to complete the Oaks–St. Leger double. The Queen also finished third in the list of winning owners and second in the breeders' table.

In a courageous attempt at the Arc de Triomphe in France she had no luck but finished a good fourth to Alleged whom she had beaten in the St. Leger. In a final run of the season, she tackled the French St. Leger, which is just under two miles. Unforunately she had to survive a very long and frequently interrupted journey and did well to finish third in extremely heavy ground.

At the conclusion of the 1978 season, the Queen hopes to send Dunfermline to be mated with the 1970 Derby winner

Nijinsky who stands in the United States and later to the 1972 Derby winner Roberto.

The Queen has built up a vast knowledge of the conformation of the ideal thoroughbred, breeding and pedigrees and reads a race very well. Additionally she possesses an exceptional memory. Ever since the days when the foals were sent over to Ireland she has taken photographs of them which enabled her to identify Doutelle from Agreement as a yearling when they returned having lost the name plates from their headcollars.

The Royal Studs at Sandringham and Wolferton in Norfolk and at Polhampton form one of Great Britain's leading establishments and are the Queen's special and very private interest. The first Royal Stud was founded at Hampton Court in the sixteenth century by Henry VIII to breed horses to hunt with the Royal Buckhounds and also to race, although these were not thoroughbreds.

The first stallions on which the thoroughbred was founded did not arrive until over 100 years later. In 1616 King James I bought the Markham Arabian, but this horse failed to found a lasting male line and it was not until Charles II (1660–85) sent his Master of the Horse, Sir John Fenwick, to the East to buy "Royal mares," that the first steps were taken to establish the breed by the importation of the Byerly Turk, the Darley Arabian in 1705, and the Godolphin Arabian in 1729.

Henry VIII, Queen Elizabeth I, James I, Charles I and Charles II all raced their own horses. When the Hampton Court Stud was closed down in 1650 under the Commonwealth, Charles II established a stud at Tutbury in Staffordshire. During the reign of William and Mary (1689–1702) Hampton Court was reopened. During Queen Anne's reign (1702–14) the paddock lay-out was enlarged. Neither George I or George II showed much interest in the turf, but the latter's son, the Duke of Cumberland, bred the renowned Eclipse in 1764.

George IV was a leading owner and won the 1788 Derby with Sir Thomas. The first Derby winner who was bred at the Royal Studs was Moses who won in the colors of H.R.H. The Duke of York.

Although less keen on racing, William IV (1830–37) was much interested in the stud at Hampton Court. On his death it was dispersed but then reformed in 1850 at the instigation of Albert, the Prince Consort.

Queen Victoria (1837–1901) did not race and each year the yearlings were sold at an auction arranged by Messrs. Tattersalls. Would-be buyers drove down the twelve miles from Hyde Park Corner by coach. The senior partner of Tattersalls conducted the sales in a circle formed by the coaches.

Stallions at Hampton Court in the 1850s and 1860s included the Derby winner Orlando. The highest fee charged for a nomination at this time was fifty guineas.

In 1887 two outstanding foals were born at Hampton Court; Sanfoin, a beautiful little chestnut colt by Springfield out of Sanda, won the Derby, while the brown filly Memoir by St. Simon out of Quiver won the Oaks and St. Leger.

The Prince of Wales then established stud farms at Sandringham and Wolferton in the 1880s under the management of Lord Marcus Beresford which were to maintain the history of the Royal Stud, and in 1894 there was a dispersal sale at Hampton Court. At one of the final Hampton Court Sales, Memoir's full sister, La Flèche, a small, light-framed filly, was sold for 5,500 guineas, a price considered so vast that Mr. Edward Tattersall called for three cheers for the purchaser, Baron de Hirsch. She was trained by John Porter at Kingsclere and was unbeaten as a two-year-old. She won the One Thousand Guineas and Oaks and would have won the Derby had not her jockey, George Barrett, who was already showing signs of insanity, ridden an appalling race. She beat her Derby conqueror Sir Hugo in the St. Leger by two lengths and when five won the Ascot Gold Cup.

The first Sandringham mare to achieve fame was Perdita II. She produced three colts by St. Simon, Florizel II, Persimmon and Diamond Jubilee. All three had very successful racing careers: Persimmon, foaled in 1893, won the Derby, St. Leger and Ascot Gold Cup; Diamond Jubilee, foaled in 1897, won the Triple Crown.

All three were at stud at Sandringham and Wolferton at a fee of 300 guineas. Florizel II sired the Derby winner Volodyovski and Persimmon had an enormous success with the filly Sceptre who won every Classic race and must rate as an all-time great.

In 1908 tragedy struck when Persimmon died of a fractured pelvis at Sandringham. He had already been leading sire on four occasions and still had several years of useful life ahead of him. He is commemorated by a huge bronze on the lawn outside the Sandringham Stud.

George V maintained the Stud with great interest. One of the best horses he bred was Scuttle, the 1926 One Thousand Guineas winner.

Feola, the filly bought in 1934, was to prove a most important acquisition. By Friar Marcus out of Aloe, she ran second in the One Thousand Guineas and third in the Oaks and went on to found one of the world's most influential thoroughbred families. Her daughters include the Classic winner Hypericum and dams of Round Table, Aureole, Doutelle and Above Suspicion, the Argentinian champions Sideral, Siderea and Sagittaria and the grand dams of Highclere and Ben Marshall.

During George VI's reign (1936–52) the foundations were being laid for one of the most successful periods in the Royal Stud's history. At this time Captain Cecil, later Captain Sir Cecil Boyd-Rochford, trained the royal horses. The greatest achievement was Hypericum's (Hyperion-Feola) victory in the 1946 One Thousand Guineas. In 1949, Feola's daughter Above Board won the Yorkshire Oaks and in 1950 she won the Cesarewitch.

In the first year of the Queen's reign, Stream of Light won the Yorkshire Oaks, the first of over fifty Pattern races to be won in the next quarter of a century by horses bred by Her Majesty. The following year, just four days after her Coronation, Aureole (Hyperion–Angelola) finished second in the

A smiling Queen greets winning jockey Joe Mercer as he leaves the winners' enclosure after his triumph in the 1974 Thousand Guineas on Highclere. Behind, Michael Oswald, to the right, Lord Porchester.
PHOTO: SPORT AND GENERAL

Derby; then at the Royal Ascot Meeting, Choir Boy won her the Royal Hunt Cup.

In the following year, 1954, Aureole established himself as the best horse in Europe winning the Coronation Cup, the Hardwicke Stakes and King George VI and Queen Elizabeth Stakes. He was then retired to the Wolferton Stud where he stood for twenty years. He was twice champion sire. His offspring won over £1 million. They included St. Crespin III, winner of the Prix de l'Arc de Triomphe, St. Paddy, winner of the Derby and St. Leger and the St. Leger winners Aurelius and Provoke. His grandson, Vaguely Noble, became one of the leading international sires in the late 1970s.

During the second half of the 1950s a continuing stream of top class horses twice put the Queen at the head of the list of winning breeders. Doutelle won good races and, retiring to Sandringham, sired such horses at Pretendre, Fighting Ship and Canisbay before dying after only four seasons. Pall Mall won the 1958 Two Thousand Guineas then retired to a successful career at stud in Ireland. Alexander, Restoration and Sierra Nevada were other major winners, and Almeria was the leading staying filly of her generation.

The 1960s were a comparatively lean period for the Royal Stud. 1965 was an exception when Canisbay (Doutelle–Stroma) won the Eclipse Stakes. After first going to Sandringham Stud, Canisbay was exported to Italy where he has already been leading sire.

1960s winners included Agreement, Apprentice, Amphora, Galois and Castle Yard. In the 1970s the Royal Studs were again most successful. Almeria's high class progeny came to the fore. Her son, Magna Carta, won the Ascot Stakes and Doncaster Cup of 1970, while her daughter, Albany, a dual winner in 1971, is already proving herself a successful brood mare.

As well as Albany, the achievements of the fillies Example, Highclere, Escorial, Joking Apart and Dunfermline have been significant in the past decade and have been a pointer to the Royal Stud's likely successes in the 1980s. In the 1970s the bay Highclere by Queen's Hussar out of Hypericum became the first filly trained in England or Ireland to win over £100,000 ($200,000) in a single year.

In 1975 the filly Joking Apart who inherited the toughness of her sire Jimmy Reppin finished third in the One Thousand Guineas and had few equals of her age over seven furlongs.

Dunfermline, the bay filly by Royal Palace out of Canisbay's half-sister Strathcona, is probably the best racehorse ever to carry the Queen's colors. Immediately after her great St. Leger victory, her two-year-old half-sister Tartan Pimpernel won the important May Hill Stakes. Dunfermline ended her three-year-old career as the best filly in Europe and the only horse ever to have beaten Alleged.

Today approximately twenty mares are kept and nearly all

are Pattern race winners, daughters or half-sisters to Pattern race winners. The main families represented are those of Feola, Avila and Young Entry. The families of Canisbay's dam Stroma and Blenheim's dam Malva are also represented.

All the mares on returning from being covered are kept at Sandringham and Wolferton. The two stud farms on the Royal Estate at Sandringham have large especially well-sheltered paddocks, mostly boarded eight feet high with split larch. Most of the buildings are made of the small pieced attractive golden-red colored carr ironstone which is quarried locally. The boxes have the space and the insulation that was a feature of those built toward the end of the last century.

Both Sandringham and Wolferton house a stallion and, during the season, his visiting mares. Until recently, the Irish Derby and St. Leger winner Ribero stood at Sandringham and he will be replaced as soon as a suitable stallion can be found.

Bustino (Busted–Shipyard) stands at Wolferton. The property of a syndicate, he won the St. Leger and as a three-year-old proved himself one of the best of his generation. Bustino's sire, grandsire and great grandsire have all been champion sires. He comes from the illustrious family of Rosetta and it will be surprising if he does not emulate his ancestors and produce more Classic winners and successful stallions.

Her Majesty takes a very close interest in the Royal Studs. She is normally in residence at Sandringham for the whole of January when she spends some time at the Studs. It would be no exaggeration to say that she is never happier than when at her Norfolk home with her family, close to her horses. Despite her heavy official schedule, she usually manages to fit in two visits to see her foals, one in the spring and one in the July–August period before they are weaned.

Michael Oswald became the Queen's Stud Manager and Lord Porchester Racing Manager in 1970 in succession to Mr. Richard Shelley. Each spring the Queen initiates the basic framework for the following year's mating plans and after several meetings with Lord Porchester and Mr. Oswald about 80 percent are firmly outlined and agreed. These are naturally subject to developments during the racing season, late foals and the way the year's crop develops. These plans are finalized toward the end of the year.

When the Queen visits her trainers, she also calls in at Polhampton, some two miles south of Kingsclere, to see her yearlings. The Stud groom is Michael Norris. The advantage of having her yearlings close to their eventual trainers is that they can be learning about their future charges' characteristics from an early age and also that some of the veterinary care has continuity.

In 1977, the Queen was Great Britain's most successful single owner, a great tribute to her skill and knowledge as, during the past quarter of a century, she has steered the Royal Stud on an ever-ascendant course against the world's top partnerships and enterprises.

The impetus and contribution she has given to the British, and indeed the world's equestrian enthusiasts cannot be overestimated and it is a pleasurable thought that it has been her relaxation and joy to do so.

Her Majesty has described her involvement with that greatest of all horses, the thoroughbred, thus, "My philosophy about racing is simple. I enjoy breeding a horse that is faster than other peoples' and that is a gamble from a long way back. I enjoy going racing, but basically I love horses and to me a thoroughbred epitomizes a really good horse. My particular hope for the future, like all breeders of horses, is to breed the winner of the Derby."

Barbara Tatlow

Sidesaddle Rider

THE ART OF riding sidesaddle is in part a legacy of a more spacious and gracious age. Today, most horsewomen ride astride, regarding sidesaddle as a remnant of the past. To them the sidesaddle appears far less secure although, in fact, it is the reverse; the sidesaddle rider is locked into her seat and less likely to fall, whereas the other relies on grip and balance.

In an emergency, if riding sidesaddle a woman may remain on her horse whereas a man riding astride would come to grief. If both were riding astride, by virtue of his strength, the man would probably stay on, whereas the woman would fall off because she has not the same muscular strength as the average man.

Even as late as the 1930s it was not unusual for several of the field in a ladies' point-to-point to ride sidesaddle. When Mrs. Christopher White won many races in the Aldershot area with her horse King Street serious accidents were infrequent. Today if just one woman rode sidesaddle in a race there would be a furore at the paddock side.

Many women who ride sidesaddle agree that the most important reason for riding in this way is that it ensures a firmer seat, which therefore makes for better hands because they should be independent of the seat. This, in turn, enables the rider to have a longer rein, which horses like, and allows her to be mounted on stronger and better horses regardless of their width.

The more secure seat has saved many falls. Clothes worn for the sidesaddle are more comfortable and certainly more elegant

The elegant combination of Mrs. Barbara Tatlow and the champion show-hack Shalbourne Last Waltz. PHOTO: PHOTONEWS

while the veil gives warmth in cold weather and controls unruly hair. In the shires today, ladies of over seventy years old can be seen out hunting, deriving confidence from the sense of security given by their sidesaddle seat. The main disadvantage is that falls are often bad ones because it is far harder for the sidesaddle rider to get clear than the astride rider.

Many horses go more kindly in a sidesaddle. They usually take to it immediately and come to like it so much that a man may well have an appalling ride on them afterward. A good shoulder and withers are a top priority; well-proportioned quarters and correct movement should give a balanced and smooth ride.

There have been many fine sidesaddle riders in the hunting

field. Between the wars Mrs. Oliver Gilbey (Bicester), Lady Fortescue and Lady Earle of Bagrave Hall, who hunted with the Quorn and all the Leicestershire packs, were outstanding. More recently, exceptional exponents include the late Lady Stanier, Lady Margaret Fortescue, Mrs. Arthur Gemmell, Lady Arbuthnot (Buccleuch Hunt in Scotland), the Countess of Feversham (Sinnington Hunt in Yorkshire) and the Duchess of Beaufort who only hunts sidesaddle.

The late Mrs. Archer-Houblon who taught the Queen and was her understudy at Trooping the Color for twenty-one years was another superb sidesaddle rider. The late Lady Leigh first rode astride and then in her early twenties was most unfortunate to have her left leg amputated below the knee following an accident when she fell against a tree. Lord Leigh suggested an off-side sidesaddle and had this made by Champion and Wilton. Lady Leigh readjusted well and displaying much courage was able to resume the sport she loved so well. She was still able to employ her left thigh to grip and to support her.

When Lady Leigh's sons were old enough to hunt, she was forced to return to riding astride because when they fell off and she had to help them it was not possible to remount sidesaddle.

Queen Alexandra had an off-side sidesaddle made up after a back injury. It can still be seen in the Royal Mews. Victorian children often learnt to ride sidesaddle with a detached leaping head on their saddles and two fixed heads to enable them to ride on both sides and so avoid curvature of the spine.

It is vital that the sidesaddle fits both horse and rider so correct stuffing is especially important. Ideally, the short balance girth is incorporated with the main girth from the back of the saddle. This is to stop the main girth slipping forward and the back of the saddle from swinging. The saddle has a fixed head on top and a leaping head on the side. These are the two curved supports into which the right and left legs respectively are placed. Whereas an astride saddle weighs about 11 lbs., a sidesaddle weighs 20 lbs.

Barbara Tatlow was a successful show and point-to-point

rider with much experience in the hunting field long before she first sat on a sidesaddle. After only a few years' practice, she is one of Britain's foremost exponents of the art of sidesaddle riding in the show ring.

"If I'd been born two or even one generation earlier, I'm sure I'd be one of those ladies you still hear about who couldn't ride astride." There are several reasons for this; as her husband, top showman David Tatlow, says, "Barbara gets more out of her horses sidesaddle than she does astride, especially with our already schooled show horses."

Barbara had a very severe attack of back trouble through a number of falls incurred when riding astride out hunting. This caused her considerable pain in her hips and thighs. At this time she found that, although she might be in tears of agony on the ground, in the saddle she did not have this pain. "One of the reasons that encouraged me to continue sidesaddle was that it enabled me to continue riding during the period when I had such awful pain from my back. Riding sidesaddle keeps your back supple, and I found it far more helpful than going down to the osteopath for manipulation."

David Tatlow runs a sizeable yard of show horses, race-horses and hunters at their home at Stow-in-the-Wold and there is a continual transition of horses. It was sheer chance that the passage of one of these horses through their stables first caused Barbara to ride sidesaddle. "We just happened to have a cob and a sidesaddle arrived in the yard at the same time. The girls had a certain inclination to try the sidesaddle, never having done so before. The cob, who belongs to Miss Betsy Profumo, was beautifully mannered, so we put on the saddle and took him into the little field adjoining our house. We hacked him round and there just happened to be a cavaletti there so we thought it would be fun to have a jump. From that day onwards and during the following show season, I put a sidesaddle on a horse at whichever show I could."

When Barbara first rode, she did not feel insecure, although the cob was very round and the saddle not exactly firm on his back. "This was the summer of 1966 and, unknown to me,

David had already completed the entries for the hack classes which included the large hack Hyde Park who had done quite well at the county shows. At the Royal International Horse Show at Wembley, he rode him outside in the ashes in the qualifying round and, although he went through to the final, he hadn't behaved too well, so was unlikely to be in the first two. I think he finished fourth. Then David said he thought it would do Hyde Park good to have another class and he might as well start in the ladies class. He then said, 'I wonder if Mrs. McIntosh (who regularly showed sidesaddle at the time) has got a ride?' Although I'd only ridden sidesaddle once I asked, 'Why can't I ride him because at least I know him well?' He had not behaved and it wouldn't really matter what happened if I rode. I had a cut-away coat as a spare, but no top hat. So I went down to Gibsons and bought a black rug with a red binding which I thought wouldn't be wasted because they were the colors we always used point-to-pointing. I used safety pins to hold in the red binding and wrapped it round me as a skirt. My father-in-law (the octogenarian of the show hack world – Harry Tatlow) was able to tell me how to pin it. There wasn't much spare time, and when I was mounted I can well remember his saying, 'Keep that right shoulder back.' David had put in a sidesaddle sheepskin although not intended for me. I borrowed a top hat from Jennie Loriston-Clarke and was all set.

"Lady Caroline Tyrell was judging and in the preliminary class, Hyde Park decided to go reasonably well and was pulled in top in front of some decent horses. We went out to do our show which not surprisingly wasn't the best, and I was glad when it was over. As the class ended and the numbers of the horses for the final judging later in the afternoon were called out, they included Hyde Park. Lady Caroline came up to me and said with a smile on her face, 'I notice you haven't a proper outfit. We are both tall and I think mine would fit you, would you like to borrow it for the afternoon?' I very gladly accepted. I finished third.

"The experience had made me keen and luckily for me the

following season we had both the large hack Lady Teller and small hack Shalbourne Last Waltz in the stable. I won the ladies class at the Royal International and the Royal. David didn't take Lady Teller to the Royal and instead rode Good News to win the large hack class and won the small class on Last Waltz. That meant we had both horses through to the Championship, so obviously David rode the larger animal and I stayed on Last Waltz sidesaddle as the final judging was to be immediately after the ladies class. Last Waltz then went on to surprise me by winning the Championship from Lady Teller" – a memory which still brings a smile of chagrin to David's face.

One problem you encounter immediately if you want to show hacks sidesaddle is that there are very few classes; usually only four at Royal Windsor, the South of England, the Royal and the Royal International Horse Show. Another is that there are not sufficient people with the knowledge to help would-be sidesaddle riders. During these two years of showing Barbara Tatlow's husband and father-in-law were the only people she could find to help her. She recalled with pleasure an incident at the Royal International. Sybil Smith, who taught the Queen to ride, came up to Barbara as she came out of the ring, slapping her on her boot and saying, "You obviously enjoy your sidesaddle riding – I don't know who you are, but hope you don't mind me telling you something just to help." Any advice from an expert could not have been more welcome. Miss Smith continued, "Just let that leather down two holes. Your left leg is too clamped up under the pommel. You don't need any weight in your left iron, just sufficient to hold the iron there." She also commented, "I like seeing your right toe down. Who told you about that?" The answer was her father-in-law, Harry Tatlow. A glance round a sidesaddle class today reveals that modern teaching prefers the right toes up; but Barbara says, "Riding sidesaddle is all balance and straightness, rather than grip. Even riding astride, people without a natural sense of balance fall off more easily. I find it obvious that if the toe is down, you get a tightness and a line through your hip up to your spine. You can easily tell if riders have

Barbara Tatlow out hacking sidesaddle. PHOTO: JAMES R. MEAD

their toes up because then there is a poke at the front of their skirts.

"I have found that most horses will go in a sidesaddle, but that you can't always get a saddle to fit. Conformation plays a big part. Preferably you need a reasonably narrow horse with good withers and a good front. When I've put a sidesaddle on run-of-the-mill hunters at home without too much front, I've found that they often appear to have more front than they have astride. Also, if a horse tends to have a slightly low head carriage, it's surprising how you can pick it up an extra six inches far better than you ever can astride because your hands

185

are that much higher. You can do more schooling a horse side-saddle too, especially with a double bridle if the horse is slightly on its forehand. The most difficult horse to ride sidesaddle is one who carries his head high and overbent, then you have the difficulty of getting its head down."

For a top sidesaddle horse she prefers one that is almost below even the normal lightweight category, certainly at the bottom of the lightweights, to produce in the show ring. Fifield fulfills this category. He was 16.0 h.h. when Barbara first showed him in ladies classes although he eventually grew to $16.2\frac{1}{2}$ h.h.

One year she was asked to ride Margaret Griffin's champion filly Aristocrat who was produced by Roy Trigg, in ladies classes. "So many good actioned show horses throw you so much at the trot, but he was so smooth. One of the nicest horses I've sat on sidesaddle at this pace. You don't want a really extravagant mover like Bunowen." Bunowen is Mr. and Mrs. A. T. Bland's Irish-bred lightweight who was the out-standing show hunter of 1977 and ridden and produced by David Tatlow.

Her first experience hunting sidesaddle came when a very nice horse came into the yard to be sold. David said a side-saddle would fit it beautifully and so she hacked it in one for about a week. When the Heythrop were hunting locally, he suggested that Barbara hunted it sidesaddle. "I'd never hunted sidesaddle before, but he was a made and mannerly hunter, so off we went. I had never jumped him and it was the first time I really needed a bit of Dutch courage and a drink at the Meet, especially if hounds were going to fly off from the first draw, which they did.

"We were in country I knew and I went happily over the first three fences, then at the next there was a solid set of rails. The horse hit the top one, which didn't break and I was catapulted as far as I've ever been shot before. I was in the middle of the field when I stopped rolling and found the horse had galloped off. I was perfectly all right, someone caught the horse and put me back on. A few minutes later, I was riding down a lane by the late Jack Gittins who had seen the incident and he told me, 'If the horse doesn't come down, but hits a fence hard, that is the way you usually go – right away!' "

Just three fences later, she experienced the other much more dangerous type of sidesaddle fall. She was second to jump a wall onto the road right behind international show-jumper Richard Sumner. The surface was just like glass, the horse landed perfectly, took one stride and his forelegs slid away and he was down and his rider underneath him. This is the most dangerous fall because both of the rider's legs are one side so invariably the horse goes down that side. The fall would have happened astride just the same, but was far worse sidesaddle. However, on this occasion, all was well, the pair got up unhurt and continued to enjoy one of the best hunts of the season, jumping about forty more fences with no further falls.

With rising costs, buying habits has become an expensive exercise. Barbara's full habit was given to her by an owner and was dark navy, a color which is more flattering to most riders than black or the variety of browns and greens that have begun to appear in Ladies Side-Saddle Association Equitation classes. In 1978, new sidesaddle outfits of coat, aprons and breeches cost approximately $600.00.

Saddles have also leaped in price and there are few saddlers who can make them today. Champion and Wilton, F.W. Owens & Co. and Mayhews are regarded as the best of the pre-war makers.

Even for those not interested in the show ring, horses are likely to go better for sidesaddle riders. As Barbara says, "At least it's one form of riding that the ladies can enjoy and the men can't, which is a great thing." It is a pity there is no major incentive, such as an Olympic medal or World Championship petition and one of the most elegant of all equestrian activities. to aim at but it is a very pleasant pastime even without competition and one of the most elegant of all equestrian activities.

The Bullen Sisters

Equestrian Family

THERE HAVE BEEN many sisters who rode and rode well, but none have reached such heights as the three Bullen sisters – Jennie Loriston-Clarke, Jane Holderness-Roddam and Sarah Bullen.

The late Colonel and Mrs. John Bullen had three daughters and three sons and, although they did not live to enjoy all their family's achievements to the full, theirs remains the only family to have produced three Olympic riders in the same generation.

Michael Bullen was a member of the British Olympic Three Day Event Team in Rome in 1960 when he rode the late Colonel V. D. S. Williams' Cottage Romance. In 1968, Jane was part of the British team which won the team gold medals at the Mexico Olympics and Jennie rode Mrs. Steele's Kadett in the British Olympic dressage team at Munich in 1972 and Montreal in 1976.

The family, who are descended from the luckless Anne Boleyn, the second of Henry VIII's wives, were brought up at Catherston Manor, near Charmouth in Dorset, with views across to the nearby sea. Their father, John Bullen, a former Royal Artillery Officer, had always hunted; while their mother, Anne, who was an extremely talented equestrian artist, had earlier run her own small circus performing with her pony Darkie, while her sister taught her dogs various tricks.

The Bullens founded the Catherston stud, and, inevitably, all the children rode. It was not long before the fields surrounding the stone house were filled with almost 100 ponies. They

The Montreal Olympics. Jennie Loriston-Clarke on Kadett.
PHOTO: LESLIE LANE

included several of the top brood mares such as the palomino Bubbly by the well-known small thoroughbred stallion Potato and out of Sunday, a Welsh mountain pony mare. Bubbly arrived at Catherston as a two-year-old, won many championships at the National Pony and Ponies of Britain Shows and was hunted by Jennie as a four-year-old.

Other stallions included Bwlch Zingaree, a brother of Bwlch Zephyr, and Xenocles, a thoroughbred stallion who is now at Jennie's Black Knoll Stud in Hampshire. In their turn, all six children, Anthony, Michael, Jennie, Charlie, Jane and Sarah showed and won at the big shows on Catherston produced ponies.

Jennie's top show pony was Miss Sylvia Calmady-Hamlyn's Royal Show, which was a gift to her when it was a three-year-old. After riding a constant string of winning show ponies, Jennie progressed onto hacks, many of them owned, as they still are, by Miss Betsy Profumo. The best remains one of her first hacks, the black mare Desert Storm – one of the few animals exhibited in the post-war era possessing true hack quality and elegance. She was by the Anglo-Arab stallion Connetable and owned by the late Miss Alicia Stubbings.

When Colonel and Mrs. Bullen died, their horses and ponies were all moved from Didmarton in the Beaufort country to Black Knoll, Brockenhurst, in the heart of the New Forest. This was the home of Jennie who was now married to Anthony Loriston-Clarke, an engineer and lecturer who specializes in metals and plastics.

With her husband, Jennie has built up a sizable enterprise which is run with great efficiency, and the discipline essential in the care of horses is maintained. Anthony toiled over the extremely well-built loose boxes himself and the establishment now includes a splendid indoor school. There is an average of about fifty horses, twenty of which belong to the Loriston-Clarkes. Ten of these are stallions, not all of which are used. They include: Jennie's current Grand Prix dressage horse Dutch Courage, a nine-year-old by the French thoroughbred stallion Millerole, out of a Dutch Gelderlander Groningen

The World Dressage Championships, Goodwood, 1978. The three individual winners, (right to left) : Jennie Loriston-Clarke (GB) on Dutch Courage (bronze) ; Uwe Schülten-Baumer (W. Germany) on Slibowitz (silver) ; and Christine Stückelberger on Granat (gold).
PHOTO : FINDLAY DAVIDSON

mare, Higonia; Xenocles, and his Anglo-Arab son, Xenarchus; the show jumper On Guard, who is ridden by international Caroline Bradley; Catherston Nightsafe, a son of former show pony Prosperity; and two Dutch horses.

Despite her ability to find and produce a steady stream of winning show hacks, Jennie's interest has gradually transferred to dressage because it is the facet of equestrianism that she most enjoys. As an indication of this, in 1978 she showed only two hacks, both for Miss Profumo. One was the last daughter of Desert Storm, Catherston Lonely Breeze, a black four-year-old small hack who much resembles her mother.

At the end of 1977, Jennie was included in the world ratings for the first time at fifteenth and retained the British Championship. In July 1978, riding Dutch Courage, she far exceeded the hopes of her more ardent fans by finishing third in the World Dressage Championships at Goodwood, Sussex to the reigning Olympic Champion, Christine Stückelberger.

Dutch Courage is a very clever horse who needs a great deal of work before he is ready to enter the arena, but he possesses the power and strength essential to succeed in world dressage in the seventies. Jennie, who first learned from Rockowansky and rode in Germany with top trainer Schultheiss, now regularly attends the courses given for a handful of Britain's leading riders by Austrian expert, Ernst Bachinger of the Spanish Riding School of Vienna.

Despite her many achievements, Jennie is overall superlative in the field of display. There has been no rider since the war who can so hold the packed houses of the Horse of the Year Show at the Empire Pool at Wembley. She has them spellbound as she advances around the arena with a sparkling series of eye-catching half passes and a devastating extended trot.

These displays are seldom worked out in detail beforehand, but evolved with a rare degree of sensitivity and creativity moments before. She only has perhaps two or three brief rehearsals with the band shortly before the show opens. "This is how I like to ride, I can go exactly as I want. The fact that the tension of competition is forgotten makes a great difference and the music really helps. It is very important that the band should understand what I am aiming for. Sometimes, I encounter a band master with his own mind which makes it very difficult. When you ride to music you can feel the horses ease as they sense the beat and this, with the atmosphere and the crowd behind you will be a great lift. I often only have three practices before my sidesaddle display and have to admit that half the time I am amazed at how well they seem to work out."

Jennie's two daughters, Anne and Elizabeth, are already enjoying the happy country life with ponies that their mother enjoyed as a child. Anne, the elder, who will be thirteen in 1979, is already so keen on jumping and eager to take on any obstacle that she seems more than likely to follow in the footsteps of her Aunt Jane.

Jane Holderness-Roddam (née Bullen) and her Olympic Gold Medallist, Our Nobby, sail over the Elephant Trap at Badminton.
PHOTO: LESLIE LANE

Jane Holderness-Roddam who, as Jane Bullen, was Britain's first lady event rider to win an Olympic gold team medal at Mexico in 1968. PHOTO: FINDLAY DAVIDSON

Jane was referred to as "the galloping nurse" by the popular daily papers when she became the first lady event rider to win a gold team medal in Mexico.

With as illustrious a sister as Jennie, it would have been easy for Jane and Sarah to have been overshadowed in a less remarkable family. Jane was a member of the Beaufort Hunt in the era that also produced no less than internationals Captain Mark Phillips and Michael Tucker. Following the Duke of Beaufort's hounds over the solid stone walls that abound around Badminton, the scene of one of her greatest triumphs, was a vital asset in her formative years as a cross-country rider.

Few could conceive training at the Middlesex Hospital and

then working as a full time nurse and simultaneously training and riding a horse to win the exacting Badminton Three Day Event. This Jane did in 1968 on her former hunter, Our Nobby. The victory secured her Olympic team place and subsequent gold medal.

Even more arresting was her return to the top of the sport a decade later on Warrior, a horse Jane had bought on behalf of American enthusiast Mrs. Suzy Howard from John Shedden. After winning the Burghley Three Day Event in 1976, Jane, now married to Tim Holderness-Roddam, returned to the Marquis of Exeter's beautiful estate in September 1977 as a member of the British team. This team recaptured the European Championship for the first time since 1971. No lady rider, and few men, have ever returned to the top of this sport after so long a period searching for the right horse. Jane is the first to give credit to Jennie, who keeps and helps prepare her sister's horse trials horses at Black Knoll.

Jane, who now lives in London, followed an exacting regime when training for the 1977 European Championships because she was then still working part-time at the Middlesex Hospital. It is ninety miles from Jane's Chelsea home to Brockenhurst and most days Jane completed the 180-mile round trip to school her horses in order to put in some time nursing at the Middlesex. In 1978, after securing a place in the team to contend the World Championships at Lexington, Kentucky by winning Badminton on Warrior, she curtailed her nursing and concentrated entirely on training her event horses.

Both Jane and Sarah followed the family pattern showing ponies until they had reached the sixteen-year-old age limit.

The three Bullen sisters, Jennie, Jane and Sarah were affectionately nicknamed Big Dog, Little Dog and Pup by their parents. "Thank goodness, Big Dog and Little Dog didn't stick," laughed the former Little Dog, middle sister Jane, but Sarah is still called "Pup" by her family and friends.

"Pup's" talents and ambitions also extended into the world of opera singing and drama and she spent some time training as an opera singer in Rome. Now she has a growing reputation

The British Chef d'Equipe, played by Anthony Hopkins, illustrates a point to Sarah Bullen in the movie International Velvet.

as a rising star of stage and television with several successful appearances to her credit. She had a starring role in M.G.M.'s *International Velvet*, directed and written by Bryan Forbes, which had its London premiere in July 1978, with stars Tatum O'Neal, Nanette Newman and Anthony Hopkins, a movie about international event riding.

Throughout she has maintained her interest in horses whenever her acting commitments have permitted and in the mid-seventies she was very successful with Mr. and Mrs. T. C. Quinney's most consistent lightweight and working hunter, Fidelio. He is a chestnut Anglo-Arab who well matched his graceful rider.

Now either Jane or Sarah fill in very adequately for Jennie on her show hacks if ever she is competing elsewhere in the now more important dressage contests.

This already tight-knit family with very diverse personal interests has become more closely united by a common bond – the love of the horse.

Racehorse Women

FROM A WOMAN'S POINT of view, the opportunities available in racing have altered irrevocably and beyond recognition since World War II. These changes, it must be recorded, did not come about without a dire and prolonged struggle by a band of pioneer women who have broken inconceivable barriers.

All women associated with racing name Mrs. Florence Nagle, now an octogenarian and living at Petworth in Sussex, as the person who initiated their breakthrough and the subsequent development of female emancipation in the sport of kings.

For years she was one of the women refused a training license. Accordingly, she was, as she described her position in 1966, "Living a lie." This wealthy great-grandmother, the daughter of Sir George Watson who founded the Maypole dairies, had to resort to having her license made out in the name of a male employee, William Stickley, whom she originally employed as a farm worker and who had become her head lad.

At the time the resourceful and determined Mrs. Nagle said, "To get into the racecourse stables, I have to be armed with an employee's card, if you please, like the stablemen do. I'm an employee of myself, and my man, whom I employ, he employs me. The whole thing is so absurd, it's almost difficult to talk sanely about it."

At the time the few women trainers in the game were by no means green. They included Miss Norah Wilmot, Mrs. Louie Dingwall, who was still training and riding her horses on the

Mrs. Florence Nagle – doyen lady of the turf. PHOTO: KEYSTONE
PRESS AGENCY

sea shore in Dorset when in her eighties, Mrs. Rosemary
Lomax, who trained in the name of her husband Ian, and Mrs.
Helen Johnson-Houghton, twin sister of the trainer Fulke
Walwyn, who trained under the name of her son, also Fulke.
Supplied with equal caliber horses they would have been well
able to take on the men on their own terms, and capable of
dealing with dopers just as well as men.

Mrs. Nagle then said: "The present group of women
trainers have reached the years of discretion. We're old and
long in the tooth. None of us is fluffy, exciting or anything

like that. We are just plain, down-to-earth, hard-working people."

She had sufficient financial resources to make a doughty stand against this sham situation and first applied for a license in the 1950s when, she said: "The only real qualification for getting a training license seems to have been a pair of trousers.

"If you give orders as a trainer, as I do, you should be held responsible if anything is wrong. Under the present system, I am not. It's a very long and lonely business fighting the Jockey Club, but the principle is my concern."

Finally on July 28, 1966, after twenty years of campaigning, she won her fight to train racehorses in her own name when settlement was announced in the Queen's Bench Division of her legal battle to compel the Jockey Club to grant her a trainer's license.

This legal victory gave her at least as much satisfaction as any race win and she said, "This was a matter of principle. I am a feminist. I believe in equal rights for women. Things should be decided by ability, not sex."

The newly recognized women trainers failed, however, to celebrate their momentous victory with a series of wins; in fact, subsequently, most went through a singularly lean period. By far the most successful that season was Miss Auriole Sinclair who had registered five wins as an officially recognized trainer by November 22, 1966.

Miss Sinclair's early life did not suggest she would become a trainer of racehorses. She was born in Rangoon where her father was a director of the Burma Grain Rice Company and the family remained there during World War I.

When her father was transferred to the London head-quarters of his company she came to England and grew up at Cowden in Sussex. The family had earlier associations with the East as in 1895 her grandparents had left their Aberdeen home and emigrated to Ceylon where they first grew coffee, which failed, and then became some of the earliest and most successful tea planters.

Miss Sinclair learned to ride and before World War II

became friendly with and rode work for Jim Geering, who had a yard at Pyecombe in Sussex.

During the war she worked as a nurse in the operating theater of the National Hospital for Nervous Diseases in Queen's Square, London.

The war over, she went back to Pyecombe and worked as an assistant for Jim Geering who had both flat and National Hunt horses and she built up an interest in pony racing. Eventually he suggested she should start her own yard, which she ran from 1948–50 at Pyecombe. Her ponies were immediately successful, registering sixty wins at a time when the main centers were Shirley Park, Birmingham, and Hawthorn Hill.

She then changed to flat horses and moved to Heath House near Lewes where she trained until 1977 when she moved to nearby Nunnery Stables; both have well-constructed eighteenth-century racing yards.

Commander and Mrs. Dawson-Miller who lived at East Hoathly offered her half-a-dozen flat horses and, "That was the start of my racing career proper; they won practically every time out and I trolleyed on from there." Her license was first held in the name of Frank Goldshaw and subsequent head lads have been John Bolton and Mick Goswell.

Miss Sinclair was granted her trainer's license two weeks after Florence Nagle and, fittingly, scored a double the very same day at Folkestone. She said, "The lady trainers of today owe everything to Mrs. Nagle. She spent an enormous amount of money and time over a period of twenty years fighting our cause with tremendous spirit. If it were not for her, we should still be carrying on with head lads."

In 1953 she had two jumpers for the Dawson-Millers: Regal Ruby won for Mrs. Dawson-Miller and News of the World won for Commander Dawson-Miller. From 1966–77 she was the leading female trainer, a position now taken over by Mrs. Rosemary Lomax, who has some high-class flat horses.

In 1978, Miss Sinclair, who has had as many as forty horses in training, had approximately twenty. She is made of stern material and in 1973 had a bad accident when a young horse

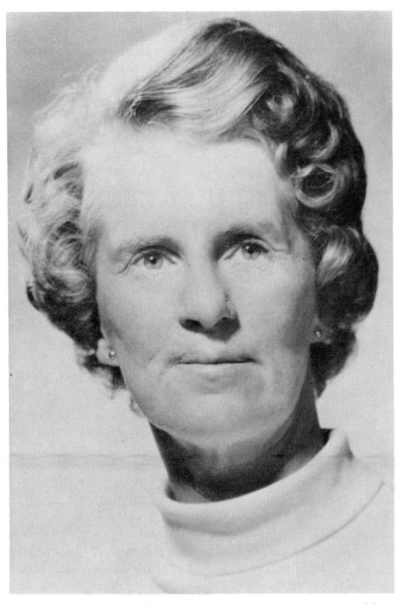

Miss Auriole Sinclair, the trainer who celebrated the granting of her license by scoring a double the very same day. PHOTO: UNIVERSAL PICTORIAL PRESS

she was riding on the downs reared up and came over backward. "I broke my arm, some ribs went through my lungs and my head was bashed in. I spent a night in the intensive care unit at Brighton Hospital then, to the rage of the surgeons, transferred myself to the osteopath Bill Tucker in London. The ambulance wouldn't take me and the osteopath nearly fainted on sight. I spent two months at his clinic in London, and when I had two lung hemorrhages they put me into the deep freeze to stop the bleeding. This knocked me sideways for two years. Only now in 1978 am I riding properly again; I had to go to the gallops in a car for a long time."

Her many winning horses include Magic Boy. Commander Dawson-Miller sent her to Ireland to buy two yearlings in the 1950s; he had always wanted an Ascot winner and the sprinter Magic Boy duly obliged and won the Wokingham Stakes at Royal Ascot.

The mare Wilhelmina Henrietta was a special favorite. By the Irish Derby winner Chamier, her name was inspired by her breeder, Mrs. W. H. Watts', initials. She was out of the French mare Thébaine and foaled when her dam was twenty-three years old. Wilhelmina Henrietta won the Bass Worthington Hurdle at Sandown, Rosebery Handicap at Kempton and became a very good hurdler winning races in 1963, 1964 and 1965. She ran twice in the Champion Hurdle at Cheltenham, where the first time she was well placed, and the second, dropped dead two hurdles from home.

Miss Sinclair favors horses of Wilhelmina Henrietta's family as they have been prolific winners and have to date given her thirty-two victories. Well-known members included Quentin Durward, who won on the flat and over hurdles, the mare Autumn Poem, who has also bred winners, the recently retired Brantridge Farmer, who became a good chaser, and Champers Galore. With such a record it is not surprising that this family is close to her heart, and she still has a few yearlings of the same line at Nunnery Stables.

Other good horses have included the two-mile chaser Simeon who won the Massey Ferguson Gold Cup, Lord Blackford's

Avec Moi, who won the Lloyds Bank Champion Novice Hurdle, Gobion Goblin, the mare Arctic Actress, who achieved the distinction of beating Cheltenham Gold Cup winner The Dikler by fifteen lengths at Lingfield, and chasers Bel et Bien and Mr. Mouse.

She cannot remember the number of races she has won and said, "As a woman trainer in what had hitherto been a man's world, I have experienced no difficulties whatsoever other than the intense irritation of having to train under the name of my head lads."

It was a natural progression for women to be allowed to ride on the flat, but it took a further six years until in 1972 the Jockey Club first allowed them to compete. There were twelve races and Meriel Tufnell became the first leading lady rider with three wins from twelve rides.

By 1974 there were forty-eight races on the flat in which women could ride and this was also the first season in which they were given permission to ride against men in a certain number of races, in which, of course, their male opponents had to be amateurs. A continuing problem is that there is a vast gulf between riding work and gallops, and riding in a race. In a trial there are seldom more than five horses and the riders are usually told exactly how they are to proceed; and the riders do not have to counter the tactics of opponents. There is no question that the women are keen, earnestly watching movies of races to study tactics and style, but there is no substitute for the first-hand experience of race riding.

Hard pullers soon hit the front in women's races which are usually run at a terrific pace. Women riders have argued that they should be allowed to ride in apprentice races but there are few who could make the weights and it is not certain that those who could would have the necessary strength to settle over-keen horses. As there are all too few opportunities for apprentices anyway, trainers would be unlikely to wish to take rides away from boy apprentices. There are a series of races in Europe, but essentially the expense of competing and availability of rides is a factor here. Sue Horton (formerly Aston) the prolific point-to-point winner won over fifty flat races on the Continent and Mrs. Ruth Hegard, the 1973 Norwegian and Reserve European Champion, who had her own stable of horses near Oslo, rode many winners.

The greatest problem remains obtaining rides in races. There are almost double the number wanting to ride as the number of those who have already ridden. Owners and trainers remain reluctant to risk their horses. An English rider has yet to emerge and win the same opportunities against professionals as Robyn Smith has in the United States.

Linda Goodwill, champion in 1973 with four wins from ten rides, a rider of some style with the knack of getting horses to run for her, was the first rider to be granted a professional license and the first to win an amateur race against men. Although she had the advantage of riding out daily with her father, trainer Arthur Goodwill, this was an astonishing demonstration of guts and endurance because as a child she suffered a severe attack of polio and it was thought she would remain an invalid for life.

In 1972 after the last race, the Lady Jockeys Association (L.J.A.) was founded. Miss Meriel Tufnell, who had begun to receive many inquiries about such details as accommodation, asked all the girls who had raced if they would support such an association and the answer was an overwhelming yes. Miss Dorothy Laird, who has a lifelong interest and knowledge of racing and whose grandfather owned a number of racehorses, came to help her as the first Honorary Secretary.

Miss Tufnell became the first Chairman of the L.J.A. Each year detailed newsletters are circulated. Racing members receive a list of all races and their conditions. Female jockeys need not belong in order to race but the majority do. Advice is given on taking out insurance and obtaining equipment. The L.J.A. works closely with the Jockey's Association and Jockey Club who help in any way possible.

After reading an early newsletter, Lord Leverhulme, then Senior Steward, replied, "It is most kind of you to send me a draft of the suggestions you intend to give to each lady rider

Folkestone, 1972. Meriel Tufnell (left) who made history when she won the first-ever lady jockey's race wins the second ladies' race on the same horse, Scorched Earth. CENTRAL PRESS PHOTOS LTD.

with a view to eliminating as many problems as possible. I think these suggestions are excellent and I do not think there are any amendments I wish to make."

In 1978 the L.J.A. Chairman was twenty-eight-year-old Diana Bissill, daughter of Jack Bissill who trains National Hunt horses at Enfield Hall, near Bridgnorth in Shropshire. She took over the role in August 1976 from Lavinia Ackroyd who now lives in Spain. Miss Bissill was originally elected as a Midland's Committee Member and carries out her role as a staunch supporter of equal rights for women riders with zeal

205

Kempton, 1972. Meriel Tufnell on Scorched Earth after their victory in the first-ever lady jockeys' race. CENTRAL PRESS PHOTOS LTD.

and dedication. She was also a Joint Master of the Albrighton Woodland Hunt in 1978.

One asset is her association with horses from an early age. "My first ride was on a wooly gray Shetland pony who had been in the pantomime 'Cinderella' in Birmingham. He had a dreadful temper and lived up to his name, Curry, to the full. His stage career ended when he kicked in the gilded coach during a performance and came to me." To date, Diana has ten races to her credit, mostly on the flat, and she rides principally for Pat Rohan who trains at Malton in Yorkshire. She also acts as assistant trainer to her father, riding exercise and helping with the day-to-day running of the stables.

She deals with a constant flow of inquiries from her office under the clock in the Enfield Hall Stableyard giving much needed definitive practical advice, and says, "Lester Piggott is the finest man riding today. But his style of riding perched on top with astonishingly short stirrups is not a method I would advise lesser riders to attempt to copy. The vital essentials are the same for both sexes: good hands, a sensitive rapport with the horse, balance and the intelligence to ride a technical race and come at the right time at the right speed.

"At this time it is best to enter as a trainer's secretary which means one is still an amateur. If one proceeds as a stable girl (which means one is being paid for exercising and grooming horses) one automatically enters a different field and loses one's amateur status. There are only ten races open to stable girls and they cannot compete in point-to-points."

In the seven years since they were first allowed to race on the flat, ladies have come a long way. The other champions have been 1974, Brooke Saunders, 1975 and 1977, Elaine Mellor, and 1976, Diana herself. In mid-1978 Marie Tinkler was putting up a strong challenge to win the title for the first time.

The facilities vary beyond belief and good ones are not invariably associated with successful or fashionable racecourses. Some committees are far keener to have women riders than others and changing rooms vary from first class to a corner of the mobile ladies' room in front of the racegoers – not very heartening on a day of drenching rain while their male rivals may be enjoying the services of a valet, drying cupboards and a cup of hot tea.

Most flat jockeys do not enjoy riding against women but are reasonably tolerant. However, as a whole, the National Hunt jockeys quite emphatically do not like it at all. Many of those to whom I spoke said they did not feel able to ride as forcefully as usual and might not always close a gap on the inside because of an innate feeling that a woman was riding in what was essentially a rough, tough, man's world. One told me, "It's a bad feeling that they might get kicked across the face and be permanently disfigured or scarred. Because of the way they are made, girls just don't fall as well as men and often sprawl in a dangerous way, especially if half the field is going to gallop over them."

Diana Bissill thinks that ladies have come a long way since their first international race was sponsored in England

Between fences during a ladies' race at the Eridge point-to-point in Sussex. PHOTO: FINDLAY DAVIDSON

by international event rider and former Amateur National Hunt jockey Chris Collins' company Goya in 1974 at Kempton Park, when twenty riders came abreast up the course. By the late 1970s Joanna Morgan from South Wales was riding well in Ireland as a professional. In March 1976, she defeated Lester Piggott in the G.T.X. Spring Handicap at Phoenix Park.

"Our assets," Diana says, "are few, except perhaps with awkward horses when we often have more patience and are prepared to try to kid them along, rather than bully a bit. Generally girls certainly take far more pride in their horses in stables than men.

"The first year we were allowed to race, everyone came to laugh at us, but since then some of the girls are getting as good as their male counterparts on the flat."

The National Hunt jockeys, struggling in perhaps the toughest sporting world, cannot be blamed for not laying down the red carpet for would-be Grand National winners on horses with theoretically no chance. Charlotte Brew was the first girl to take part in the Grand National in 1977 on her point-to-point horse Barony Fort, an adventure which received unprecedented publicity. She kept out of the way of the field and jumped all but four of the Grand National fences before ending in the ditch which guards the fourth from home. She tried several times to negotiate the obstacle but Barony Fort who had been predictably and impossibly outclassed from the start decided to call it a day.

When permission was granted for women to race under rules, the first to win a steeplechase was Diana Thorne (now Henderson) who partnered her father's Ben Ruler to beat him and Air General by a neck in the Nimrod Hunter Chase at Stratford-on-Avon on February 7, 1976.

Only weeks later, her twin sister, Jane, was in the winners' enclosure, the second lady winner on her own Indian Diva at Warwick, and two seasons later, in April 1978, Jane finished a gallant second on her father's brilliant young chaser, Spartan Missile, in a race of an entirely different caliber – the Whitbread Gold Cup at Sandown Park. Here she finished a length behind Tommy Stack on Strombolus in a race which included such class horses as Fort Devon and Master H, displaying extraordinary skill and unexpected strength for her size.

In 1978, the Countess of Halifax, Mrs. Helen Johnson-Houghton, and Mrs. Priscilla Hastings were honored and set yet another precedent when they became the first ever women members of the Jockey Club. But even then they were not social members and free to use the Club's facilities in its splendid Georgian-style house at Newmarket. Women members, the Jockey Club pointed out, could use the administrative office in London.

Show-Jumpers

GREAT BRITAIN HAS an astonishing capacity for throwing up women who can compete with and outride men in the world's major show-jumping arenas. Welsh rider Debbie Johnsey, whose curly, pale gold hair and aquamarine eyes suggest a model for Botticelli rather than the archetype lady show-jumper, is the latest to follow this tradition.

The equestrian section of the Olympics is the one sport in which men and women compete against each other, and in show-jumping, the latter have more than held their own.

Pat Smythe was the first to be allowed to compete in the Games and proved herself by winning a bronze team medal at Stockholm in 1956 on Flanagan along with Wilf White and Peter Robeson.

In the last three Olympiads, Britain has included one girl in her team and on each occasion they have outridden their team mates in the individual contest – the Grand Prix. Marion Mould and Stroller took the silver medal at Mexico City in 1968, Ann Moore followed suit with Psalm in Munich in 1972 and last year Debbie Johnsey and Moxy finished a very creditable fourth in Canada after Alwin Schockemöhle won the gold on Warwick Rex following a three-way jump-off for the silver and bronze medals. This was after a long day's jumping over what were probably the biggest courses ever set for the Olympic Games.

Debbie's precocious talent was officially recognized when she was selected for the British Junior Team at the tender age of eleven with her pony stallion Champ. However, the British

Debbie Johnsey and Moxy splash through the mud in the jump-off for the silver and bronze medals at the Montreal Olympics at Bromont in 1976. PHOTO: LESLIE LANE

Show Jumping Association had failed to check the minimum age necessary to ride in the Junior European Championships and were forced to withdraw her. Consequently her international debut was delayed until 1971 when she was fourteen.

Although still diminutive and weighing only five stone she changed from ponies to horses in 1972 and by 1973, when only sixteen, showed she had succeeded in the transition by winning the Whitbread Young Rider's title at Wembley with Speculator. The following year, she won the Junior European title with the same horse, who is by the premium stallion Specific, sire of the Grand National winner Specify, and who was brought out by Carmen Lanni in the north.

British Chef d'Equipe Ronnie Massarella keeps Debbie Johnsey's boots clean by giving her a lift over the mud at Lucerne in June, 1976. PHOTO: FINDLAY DAVIDSON

The first time I saw Debbie ride she was aged about twelve; and after her round she was standing in a flood of tears in the collecting ring at Stafford County Show with her parents. These were tears of self-incrimination and fury. She was well aware that she had made some riding errors, so Champ had lost a class he could have won.

In July 1976 at Bromont in Canada, with dark storm clouds hanging over the Laurentian Mountains, after a dramatic day's jumping, Debbie, then a slender nineteen-year-old, stood in the water-covered collecting ring with Moxy and her parents. Again she was fighting back tears of disappointment at being narrowly edged out of an Olympic medal after proving herself among the world's best in a day of momentous stress and strain few teenagers will even experience, let alone come through so well.

But these tears are far from an indication of weakness but rather an expression of one of Debbie's greatest assets, her total determination. She struggled to establish herself in the senior ranks, surviving a difficult period when Speculator was very strong and she could not control him, and was undeterred by the severely testing transitional stage which many other promising juniors experience, fail to overcome and so subsequently abandon the sport.

Another great virtue is her cool headedness in competition. The way she looks forward to the big championship and is not upset by the occasional slight mishap, singles her out from her contemporaries.

The long 1976 season only allowed a brief lay-off the following January and Debbie arrived home for Christmas to find herself acclaimed a star and collected many sporting awards during the winter. She also attended the premier of the Royal Windsor Horse Show movie which featured training and competing, and talked about her experiences during the Games over the theme music of the E.M.I. record "Come Ride with Me."

Debbie's home is Devauden Court, a white-painted, much enlarged former estate house set high above Itton, Monmouthshire with a breathtaking view across pasture land through a glen between the Shirenewton Hills and Black Chepstow Park Wood down to the Severn River gleaming in the far distance deep below the hills of Somerset in England.

Debbie is the second child of a family of four. Kevin is two years older, Clair five years younger and brother Lee eleven years younger. Despite all her achievements, Debbie remains extremely modest. At home, she has little chance to be otherwise. In the June prior to the Montreal Olympics, while Debbie fought for her Olympic place under extremely tense conditions in front of the selection committee in the grounds of Cardiff Castle, and won the final trial on Moxy, Lee whiled away the time alternately sliding down the castle fortifications on a tin tray and making mud pies in the collecting ring.

One day, not so long ago, Lee arrived home from school after talking with his classmates to query, "Have I got a famous sister?" And, when answered in the affirmative, he continued, "Which one?"

Liz Edgar jumps a spread in exemplary style on one of her favorites,

Like Ann Moore and other leading lady show-jumpers before her, Debbie has no illusions about trying to lead a full social life like her contemporaries in less demanding occupations. In the late 1970s, with the coming of sponsorship, international show-jumping has developed into a year round sport and her life is a continuing pattern of packing and unpacking, travel, competition and schooling young horses during brief periods at home, some of which may become members of her top string.

The standard is so high that no let-up is possible. The blue swimming pool set below Devauden Court looks inviting, even in the pale winter sun, but the demands of the circuit meant that during the long hot summer of 1976, she swam in it just twice.

There are, of course, compensations. Debbie has opportunities for fully paid travel as a British team rider to some of the world's most exciting cities, such as Berlin, Paris, Madrid, Rome, New York, Washington, D.C. and Johannesburg, and chances too to meet famous people from many different backgrounds. But more often than not there is little time to see much of the place in which they are competing because classes

the speed horse Everest Makedo. PHOTO: BOB LANGRISH

go on most of the day and often into the night as well.

To embark alone as a teenager on this circuit would be a formidable prospect. The recent British internationals have all enjoyed their father's support, both traveling and with their schooling. Ralph Coakes helped his daughter Marion Mould before her marriage to David Mould, who for many years was jockey to the Queen Mother; Norman Moore was his daughter Ann's adviser, trainer and constant companion whenever his business interests allowed until she retired in 1975, while Debbie's father Terry, who earlier rode in some races, fills this role for his daughter.

Unhappily, in early 1978, Debbie's 1976 Olympic partner Moxy had to be put down because of incurable lameness and he is buried in the grounds of their home. It was a severe blow for the Johnseys. They had lost not only one of the world's top international horses, which are extremely difficult to find, but also a horse who was very much a family favorite. Debbie had established the very close relationship with Moxy that seems more usual with female riders than men. When Moxy came into a strange arena, as before his superb performance at Bromont, he turned to look round at her in the

215

Checking the course before jumping. Caroline Bradley on Mr. John Harding's stallion Marius at Aachen C.S.I.O. in July, 1978.
PHOTO: FINDLAY DAVIDSON

Caroline Bradley acts as passenger to Mrs. Jonathan Dick during a Scurry Driving Competition at the Nice International Horse Show in 1978. PHOTO: FINDLAY DAVIDSON

saddle and after a reassuring pat was on his way.

In 1978, Debbie's top partner was the brilliant American horse Croupier, with whom she was nominated for the World Championships. Unfortunately he was not quite right at the critical time of final selection and so Debbie was not chosen for the World Championships at Aachen, West Germany.

Instead, she concentrated on bringing on some promising young horses, among them Puma, an American-bred registered quarter-horse, and Classic.

Debbie does not plan to stay in the sport for ever and wants before too long, "To get married and have a family, just like everyone else of my age."

When she does retire the sport will be the poorer for loss of the Welsh girl of whom Britain's top Chef d'Equipe Ronnie Massarella says, "Debbie's great asset to any team is her superb temperament." Her fellow countryman David Broome, the 1970 World Champion who lives close by and has watched

Caroline Bradley in action on Tigre at the World Championships at Aachen in 1978. PHOTO: FINDLAY DAVIDSON

her progress to an international from her early days paid her a great compliment when he told me recently, "I think Debbie's best is yet to come."

Two riders, Liz Edgar and Caroline Bradley, who both live in the same county, Warwickshire, unquestionably rated among the world's best of either sex in the 1970s although neither had competed for Olympic honors.

Liz, sister of David Broome, could have gone to the 1964 Olympics in Tokyo with Jacopo but not relishing long flights or big occasions preferred to give the ride to her brother, who finished twenty-first on him in the individual Grand Prix and was a member of the British team which finished fourth to Germany.

Before her marriage Liz enjoyed many successes on her father's mare Bess with whom she won the 1964 British Championship, and also Ballan Excelsior. Liz has exactly the same brilliant eye for a stride and the inbuilt clock in her head as her famous brother. Her father Fred Broome who taught

Mary Chapot on White Lightning during the Queen Elizabeth II Cup at the Royal International Horse Show in 1968. She was the first American to win this trophy. PHOTO: FINDLAY DAVIDSON

and trained all his family of four to ride said, "David and Liz were taught the same way and there is not much to choose between them. Liz never realized she could defeat David until one day they were in the final of the same big competition and she came to me and said, 'What can I do to beat him?' I said, 'I taught you both, just go out and do your best and you may well win.' She did and that victory brought confidence." It proved the turning point in the career of an outstanding, quiet and self-effacing rider because Liz now realized her own ability.

In the late 1970s Liz still enjoyed making young horses best but had some outstanding successes on the mostly German-bred horses owned by the Everest Stud. In 1977 she won the Queen Elizabeth II Cup at the Royal International Horse Show in July, then in November she became the first British rider to capture the Grand Prix of New York since 1967 when it was won by Harvey Smith. On both occasions her partner was Everest Wallaby.

Another major victory was the Ladies National Championship in 1975 on Everest Mayday and she also became the 1977 British Amateur Champion on Everest Wallaby at the Benson and Hedges Cardiff International. In the same year she was put on the list of possibles for the 1980 Olympic Games in Moscow with the Everest Stud's promising young chestnut gelding Everest Forever.

By 1978 her only child Maria was seven years old and already becoming a force in junior jumping with her ponies Bali and Franco. With such a promising daughter it is safe to say that in the hopefully distant day when Liz decides to retire from international competition, she will still be on the circuit enjoying guiding and helping Maria.

In 1978 when Warwickshire international Caroline Bradley was thirty-two years old, her quiet classical style and diligent schooling were finally rewarded when she finished fifth overall and the highest placed lady in the World Championships at Aachen in August on the brilliant Hanoverian-thoroughbred cross Tigre. Riding the same gray horse, whom she owns in partnership with Donald Bannocks, Caroline also captured the

Members of the U.S. Equestrian Team pose at Madison Square
Garden in New York, 1968 after winning the Nations Cup of the
National Horse Show. Left to right: Bill Steinkraus, Kathy Kusner,
Mary Chapot and Frank Chapot. The team won the coveted cup
for going over a total of ninety fences without a fault.
WIDE WORLD PHOTOS

Grand Prix of Nice and Calgary.

The best post-war Continental lady rider is unquestionably
Janon Tissot, who was born in French Indo-China in 1945
to a Chinese mother. At the time, her French father was in
charge of building highways.

When she was only nineteen she was a member of the
French team who won the silver team medals at the 1964
Tokyo Olympics on Kenavo D. Two years later she captured
the European Ladies Championship on the same horse.

In 1968 she was again a member of the French team who
won the team silver medals in Mexico, this time riding Rocket.

With Rocket she became World Ladies Champion in 1970
at Copenhagen, taking the title from Marion Mould and
Stroller. In 1973 she changed her maiden name of Lefebvre
to Tissot when she married Jean-Louis, son of Rocket's

owner. She retained the title at La Baule in 1974 since when it has not been contested.

The United States has not lagged behind where the fair sex is concerned; indeed the U.S. Chef d'Equipe and coach Bert de Nemethy, who one might imagine to be a resolute advocate of the male sex, is contrarily a staunch defender of "my girls."

To be a female rider in the United States is a rather different proposition from that in Great Britain because the team is centered on the United States Equestrian Team's base at Gladstone, New Jersey, which mean's leaving one's home for often lengthy periods of time. But Bert's girls have proved exemplary in both demeanor and style and well able to take on and beat the men.

One of the first was the former Mary Mairs, now Mary Chapot, and married to former U.S.E.T. Olympic rider Frank Chapot. In 1960 Mary won the Hunter Seat Medals Finals in Madison Square Garden and subsequently, Bert de Nemethy invited her and her chestnut mare Tomboy to train at Gladstone in the summer of 1961. He remembers her arriving from her California home with a small dog for company and settling in well. Tomboy had an exceptional temperament and did not like hitting fences. In 1962 the pair were chosen to go to Europe and were members of the United States team who won the Aachen Nations Cup. Returning home they were members of the United States team who won all three Nations Cups on the North American fall circuit.

At the 1963 Pan-American Games in São Paulo, Mary, riding Tomboy, became the first American ever to win an individual Games gold medal in equestrianism. During the following five years she became a classic stylist in the high tradition of the U.S.E.T. since it was taken over by Bert de Nemethy.

With Tomboy, who was so named because she was a rather masculine mare, Mary won many Grand Prix including those of New York, Harrisburg and Cleveland and Essen in Germany. She won the Saddle of Honor at the Royal International Horse Show in London and contributed to countless

*Kathy Kusner riding Untouchable in the International Horse Show
in Rome, 1967.* WIDE WORLD PHOTOS

Nations Cup victories.

At the end of 1968 Tomboy was retired and later produced
a foal, Good News, to Good Twist, the stallion on whom
Mary's husband Frank registered so many victories. Good
News is now at stud at their farm at Neshanic Station, New
Jersey, and so continues the line because, sadly, Tomboy was
killed soon afterward in a farm accident.

In 1968 Mary won the coveted Queen Elizabeth II Cup at
London's Royal International on White Lightning and the
same year the pair were members of the United States team at
the Mexico Olympics. Mary has now retired from international jumping and is in demand as a judge of hunter and
equitation classes.

Up to and including the 1976 Olympics, Kathy Kusner is
the only American woman rider to have won an Olympic

show-jumping medal. She achieved this on her third attempt at Munich in 1972 when riding Fleet Apple, the horse who jumped with cotton wool in his ears because the noise of the crowd upset him, when she was a member of the U.S.E.T. who won the Silver team medals.

By nature she is a wanderer who finds it hard to settle in one place for long. She has also ridden in races and for some time worked piloting jet airplanes.

Small and light boned, she has the instinctive touch of the natural horsewoman and her many successes while a member of the U.S.E.T. included finishing second in the 1965 World Championship and winning the European Championship in 1967.

Out of many horses, her greatest partnership was achieved with Untouchable, a chestnut gelding found by the late Benny O'Meara in 1962 in the Mid-West and first introduced by him to jumping when he was unbeaten in green jumper classes on the Florida circuit.

After Untouchable won the Open Jumper title at New York's National Horse Show O'Meara loaned him to the U.S.E.T. as a possible Olympic mount for Kathy. He proved to be just this, winning five major European Classes in 1964 and then finishing thirteenth in the Tokyo Olympics.

Over the next four years he won constantly for the U.S.E.T., carrying Kathy to her European Championship and also in the 1968 Mexico Olympics where the United States narrowly missed the bronze medals. Two years later he was retired.

Untouchable was a horse with a really hot temperament and Kathy remembers him as: "The best horse I've ever known he was a former race horse and had won seven races. Mentally he was pretty wild, he had a very hot temperament. I had to try to stay one move ahead of him all the time; it was like trying to solve a Chinese puzzle, I never quite sorted out all the problems he set me. His temperament would get us into the most fearful difficulties approaching a fence, and then, time after time, he'd get us safely over and on our way through sheer class and talent."